"Writing my doctoral dissertation on Thomas Goodwin, in his own Oxford, turned out to be a formative period in my spiritual life. It's not just the doctrinal logic but the pastoral rhetoric that strikes home. 'He won't do it again,' I'd resolve, but again and again he brought me to tears. Someone really put his finger on my heart. I don't agree with all of Goodwin's points, but I think anyone today would cherish him as their pastor. Andrew Ballitch has done a tremendous service by bringing Goodwin's seminal insights on assurance to a new audience—which is in many ways very comparable to his own seventeenth-century context. If you're looking for a pastor from the past who seems to know you better than you know yourself, you're in for a real treat."

—**Michael Horton,** J. Gresham Machen Professor of Theology, Westminster Seminary California

"Thomas Goodwin is gaining popularity today as a Puritan who wrote some splendid works to help believers understand the love of God for them. Goodwin's doctrine of assurance was somewhat unique in his day, but many theologians and pastors joined with him in separating the sealing of the Spirit from conversion. In this book, the reader will get a helpful introduction to these matters. Even if one does not fully agree with Goodwin, there are so many helpful pastoral insights into the nature of the Christian life in this book that it is worth reading regardless of one's position on assurance of salvation."

—**Mark Jones,** senior minister, Faith Vancouver Presbyterian Church

"By the late sixteenth century, the issue of assurance loomed large within English Reformed theology. While the Church of Rome insisted that no one can be infallibly certain of their salvation, some Protestants equated assurance with a mere speculative knowledge of Christ. Of those who spoke into the resultant confusion, Thomas Goodwin figured prominently due to his depth of analysis. For his first-rate treatment of Goodwin's position, Dr. Ballitch is to be thanked. His study sheds light not only on an important juncture in the history of English Reformed theology but on a subject that is important to all believers."

—**J. Stephen Yuille,** professor of spiritual formation and pastoral theology, Southwestern Baptist Theological Seminary, Fort Worth, TX

T0312556

"Andrew Ballitch's *Finding Assurance with Thomas Goodwin* is an excellent resource for anyone looking to familiarize oneself with Goodwin's doctrine of assurance and the sealing of the Spirit. Ballitch's writing is winsome, and he skillfully interweaves the historical account of Goodwin's life and teaching with his own beautifully pastoral observations about their significance to the modern church. Ballitch's balanced handling of the topic, noting both strengths and weaknesses of the arguments, provides space for theological reflection and conversation that will be beneficial to Christians of all denominational backgrounds."

—**Joshua H. Cook,** pastor, Our Savior Lutheran Church (LCMS), Louisville, KY

"Thomas Goodwin was a mighty Puritan expositor of the heart of Christ and the heart of man. I have personally benefited from Goodwin's writings so much that I count him a dear friend and mentor. In this book, Andrew Ballitch ably traces Goodwin's experience and doctrine of assurance of salvation. As Ballitch helps us to see, Goodwin's teaching fell within a spectrum of Puritan views of how God assures His children of His favor toward them and salvation in them. While Goodwin's exegesis and doctrine are not above criticism at times, his writings contain many biblically experiential and practical lessons for us still today."

—**Joel R. Beeke,** president, Puritan Reformed Theological Seminary

"Every believer encounters seasons of doubt. Sometimes, that doubt reaches to the core questions about our eternal destiny. Andrew Ballitch examines the life and writings of Thomas Goodwin and his struggles with doubt to bring clarity and modern application to the wonderful doctrine of assurance. Andrew brings rich insight from this historical Puritan that will benefit every believer with solid reasons for trusting the assurance the Lord provides his children."

—**David Lane,** district superintendent, Christian and Missionary Alliance

"Shepherds of God's flock would benefit from reading this book and thinking more deeply on the doctrine of assurance. Without clarity on this subject, followers of Christ are susceptible to ineffective living following their feelings and experiences rather than the truth of God's word."

—**Charlie Davis,** senior pastor, Hillcrest Baptist Church, New Albany, MS

FINDING ASSURANCE

WITH

THOMAS GOODWIN

FINDING ASSURANCE

—

WITH

—

THOMAS GOODWIN

ANDREW S. BALLITCH

LEXHAM PRESS

Finding Assurance with Thomas Goodwin
Lived Theology

Copyright 2023 Andrew S. Ballitch

Lexham Press, 1313 Commercial St., Bellingham, WA 98225
LexhamPress.com

You may use brief quotations from this resource in presentations, articles, and books. For all other uses, please write Lexham Press for permission. Email us at permissions@lexhampress.com.

Unless otherwise noted, Scripture quotations are from *ESV*® *Bible* (*The Holy Bible, English Standard Version*®), copyright © 2001 by Crossway Bibles, a publishing ministry of Good News Publishers. Used by permission. All rights reserved.

Scripture quotations marked (KJV) are from the King James Version. Public domain.

Print ISBN 9781683597223
Digital ISBN 9781683597230
Library of Congress Control Number 2023933404

Series Editor: Michael A. G. Haykin
Lexham Editorial: Todd Hains, Claire Brubaker, Cindy Huelat, Jordan Short, Mandi Newell
Cover Design: Joshua Hunt
Typesetting: Abigail Stocker, Justin Marr

To my precious children,
Elizabeth, Etta, and Winston,
May you one day enjoy full assurance of faith.

Contents

Timeline of
Thomas Goodwin's Life

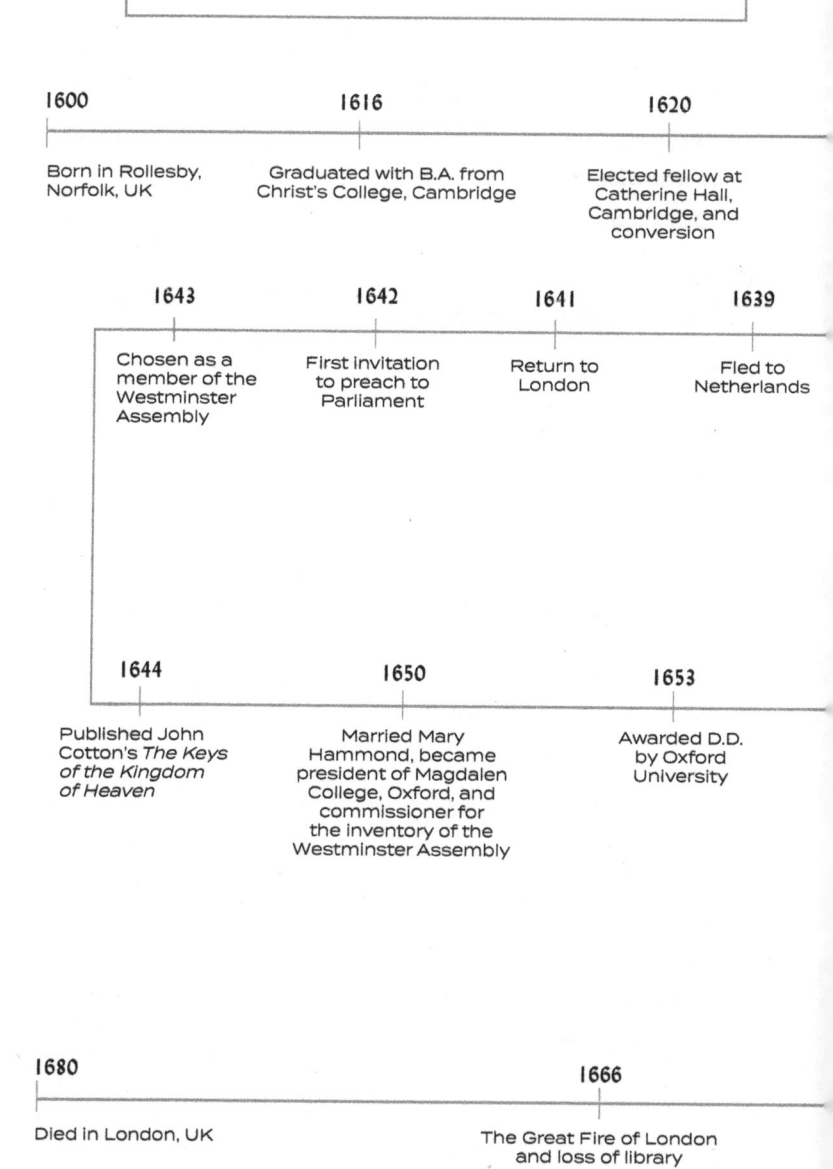

1600
Born in Rollesby, Norfolk, UK

1616
Graduated with B.A. from Christ's College, Cambridge

1620
Elected fellow at Catherine Hall, Cambridge, and conversion

1643
Chosen as a member of the Westminster Assembly

1642
First invitation to preach to Parliament

1641
Return to London

1639
Fled to Netherlands

1644
Published John Cotton's *The Keys of the Kingdom of Heaven*

1650
Married Mary Hammond, became president of Magdalen College, Oxford, and commissioner for the inventory of the Westminster Assembly

1653
Awarded D.D. by Oxford University

1680
Died in London, UK

1666
The Great Fire of London and loss of library

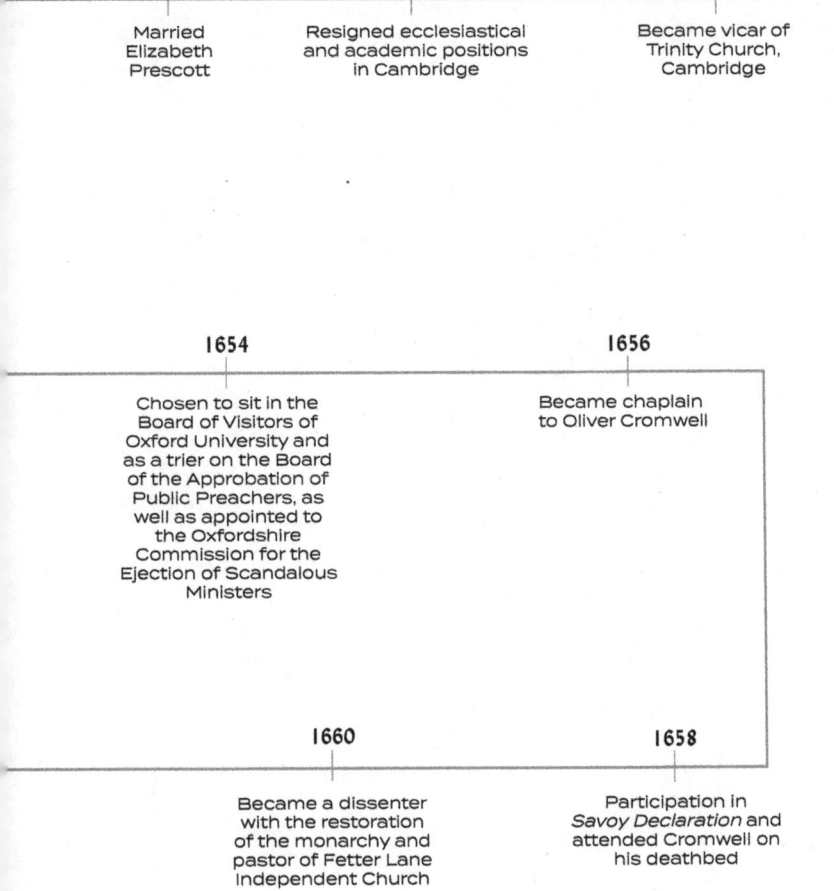

1625

Licensed to preach and became minister at St. Andrew the Great, Cambridge

1628

Became lecturer at Trinity Church, Cambridge

1638

Married Elizabeth Prescott

1634

Resigned ecclesiastical and academic positions in Cambridge

1632

Became vicar of Trinity Church, Cambridge

1654

Chosen to sit in the Board of Visitors of Oxford University and as a trier on the Board of the Approbation of Public Preachers, as well as appointed to the Oxfordshire Commission for the Ejection of Scandalous Ministers

1656

Became chaplain to Oliver Cromwell

1660

Became a dissenter with the restoration of the monarchy and pastor of Fetter Lane Independent Church

1658

Participation in *Savoy Declaration* and attended Cromwell on his deathbed

LIVED
THEOLOGY

Series Preface

Men and women—not ideas—make history. Ideas have influence only if they grip the minds and energize the wills of flesh-and-blood individuals.

This is no less true in the history of Christianity than it is in other spheres of history. For example, the eventual success of Trinitarianism in the fourth century was not simply the triumph of an idea but of the biblical convictions and piety of believers like Hilary and Athanasius, Basil of Caesarea and Macarius-Symeon. Thirteen hundred years later, men and women like William Carey, William Ward, and Hannah Marshman were propelled onto the mission field of India—their grit and gumption founded on the conviction that the living, risen Lord has given his church an ongoing command: "Go therefore and make disciples of all nations, baptizing them in the name of the Father and of the Son and of the Holy Spirit, teaching them to observe all that I have commanded you. And behold, I am with you always, to the end of the age" (Matt 28:19–20). These verses had an impact when they found a lodging-place in their hearts.

The Lived Theology series traces the way that biblical concepts and ideas are lived out in the lives of Christians, some well known, some relatively unknown (though we hope that more people will know their stories). These books tell the stories of these men and women and also describe the way in which ideas become clothed in concrete decisions and actions.

The goal for all of the books is the same: to remember what lived theology looks like. And in remembering this, we hope that these Christians' responses to their historical contexts and cultures will be a source of wisdom for us today.

> *And these all, having obtained a good report through faith, received not the promise: God having provided some better thing for us, that they without us should not be made perfect. Wherefore seeing we also are compassed about with so great a cloud of witnesses, let us lay aside every weight, and the sin which doth so easily beset us, and let us run with patience the race that is set before us, Looking unto Jesus the author and finisher of our faith.* (Heb 11:39–12:2 KJV)

Michael A. G. Haykin
Chair and Professor of Church History
The Southern Baptist Theological Seminary

Acknowledgments

Many thanks are in order upon the completion of this book. First, thank you to Michael Haykin for his investment in young scholars in general and me in particular. A book on Thomas Goodwin and the doctrine of assurance in the Lived Theology series was his suggestion over brunch in Louisville, Kentucky, back in 2018. He also generously extended an invitation to submit a proposal for the project. His openhandedness with writing opportunities has been a continual presence in my life since I had him as a professor at the Southern Baptist Theological Seminary.

Thanks also to Lexham Press for taking a chance by giving a contract to me as a first-time popular-level author. And to Todd Hains for his masterful shepherding of this effort through the extensive process of taking an idea through to publication, and for his help and encouragement each step of the way. His whole team has been a delight to work with, and special thanks goes to Rachel Welcher for her careful and insightful reading of the first draft. A team really was involved in what is before you, for which I am grateful to say this book is significantly better. The inevitable mistakes that remain are, of course, my own.

Many others have come to my aid as well, two of whom must be mentioned by name. Stephen Yuille provided me with helpful leads regarding who might be heirs of Goodwin's theology of assurance. Huafang Xu pointed me to relevant sections of the Anne Dutton corpus. Both saved me vast amounts of time.

I want to warmly express my appreciation to the elders and saints of Westwood Alliance Church for valuing my writing ministry and recognizing how it complements ministry in the local church. I trust they have seen and will continue to see the fruits of these labors in my preaching and pastoral care. After feeding my own soul, this is my primary aim in these endeavors.

Finally, I save my heartiest thank-you for my family. Much of the time spent studying Goodwin could have inevitably been spent with them. Darcy has been a tireless supporter of my research and writing throughout our marriage, encouraging me to persevere when I've needed it most. She has also proofread everything I've written, from college seminar papers to this book. It's all better for it. She is a faithful partner in all things. Our three children, Lizzy, Etta, and Winston, have been a continual source of joyful respite. It is to them I dedicate this book, praying that they would each grow up to know a most blessed assurance of salvation.

Andrew S. Ballitch
Mansfield, Ohio
2022

Introduction

The assurance of faith is a universal Christian desire, while doubt is a common Christian experience. The Puritans, perhaps more than any other group in history, were acutely aware of this reality and relentlessly probed Scripture and their own experience for comfort, and not for themselves alone but that they might share it with others in their pastoral ministries. Thomas Goodwin (1600–1680) wrestled with doubt for seven years after his conversion. When assurance came, it came with rapturous joy and euphoric confidence in that Christ died for him personally, that his sins were in fact forgiven. Such confidence endured and resulted in a life of increased holiness, usefulness in ministry, and perseverance in the faith.

Goodwin found a biblical basis for this experience in the language of the Spirit's sealing from Ephesians 1:13–14 and developed the idea of the sealing of the Spirit as a second work of grace in which the believer is convinced beyond doubt in the soul of personal salvation, a work not enjoyed by every believer but one to be sought by all. In so doing, Goodwin pushed the Puritan doctrine of assurance to its apex. As an innovative doctrine, clear in both his life and writings, the sealing of the Spirit is a fitting lens through which to view Goodwin's biography and thereby bring coherence to a story that spans some of the most eventful years in English history. This doctrine also provides help for the perennial struggle for assurance that is ever present in the lives of Christians.

LIFE AND TIMES

By 1600, England had enjoyed over four decades of relative religious peace. King Henry VIII (1491–1547) broke the Church of England away from the Church of Rome in 1534, but not for doctrinal reasons. The pope failed to provide his desired annulment of his marriage to Catherine of Aragon (1485–1536), who had not provided Henry with a male heir. His thoroughly Protestant archbishop of Canterbury, Thomas Cranmer (1489–1556), thus had to proceed slowly and cautiously with internal church reform. When Henry's son became king in 1547, everything changed. Edward VI (1537–1553) was only nine years old when he was crowned, and his regents accelerated the English Reformation. Cranmer wrote the Book of Common Prayer, designed to regulate worship in the Church of England, and what would become the Thirty-Nine Articles, the confessional standard of the national church. Edward, a sickly child, died in 1553, and his half-sister, Mary (1516–1558), ascended to power. She was the daughter of Henry's first wife, Catherine, who successfully passed down her devout Catholic faith and bitterness toward the English Reformation, which had caused her to be sidelined. Mary earned her nickname, "Bloody Mary," by burning at the stake roughly three hundred Protestants, most infamously Cranmer himself, and exiling many more in her attempt to reverse the religious course. Her reign was cut short by her death in 1558.

By the time Elizabeth I (1533–1603), Henry's last remaining heir, became queen, the country was weary of religious upheaval. A series of laws passed in 1558, known as the Elizabethan Settlement, put England on its permanent Protestant course, but some, who came to be labeled Puritans, viewed this as a compromise, which it was. At the risk of oversimplification, Elizabeth reformed the church's doctrine but not its practice. Theologically, the Church of England became truly Protestant, part of the Reformed tradition. But in terms of its externals and worship forms, much was carried over, such as kneeling to receive the sacrament of the Lord's Supper, priestly vestments, the sign of the cross, and perhaps most significantly, the church's hierarchy of bishops. To the Puritans such things smacked of superstition and Roman Catholicism, so they wanted the externals to be reformed as well. They wanted to purify the Church of England by making its worship and government look like what they saw in John Calvin's (1509–1564) Geneva and other Reformed centers on the Continent. In short, they wanted a church strictly regulated by Scripture.

This regulation was anything but a burden in the Puritan mind. In fact, it was a liberating principle. For them, only elements of worship with clear precept in Scripture or apostolic precedent belonged in the church. If Scripture regulated worship, then people would be free to worship without human impositions, whether seemingly helpful, hurtful, or indifferent. The problem, however, was that the Book of Common Prayer imposed all kinds of demands and restrictions. To make matters worse, the requirements were enforced by bishops, whose very offices were illegitimate in the estimation of most Puritans. While the Church of England would never return to the Roman Catholic fold, the late sixteenth and early seventeenth centuries saw a great deal of chafing as the Puritans worked for further reformation.

In this context, Goodwin was born in 1600 to Puritan parents in Rollesby, Norfolk. The county was infamous for its nonconformity to the worship dictated by the Book of Common Prayer and its resistance to religious persecution by the Crown. Goodwin's Puritan parents raised him religiously and determined that he would pursue the ministry of the gospel. They provided him with an education, including in Greek and Hebrew, and sent him to Christ's College, Cambridge, at the age of fourteen. He matriculated to Catherine Hall, Cambridge, in 1620, where he became a fellow and lecturer. While he had experienced conviction of sin as early as age six, knew the gospel, and had several obvious seasons when the Lord was working in his life spiritually, it was 1620 when he was truly saved, beginning his seven-year struggle for assurance. In addition to his university work, he gained a preaching license in 1625. He ministered at St. Andrew the Great and eventually at Trinity Church starting in 1628, the church known for its pastors Richard Sibbes (1577–1635) and John Preston (1587–1628). He followed their precedent of plain-style Puritan preaching and was later honored with appointment as one of the editors of Preston's sermons. He was also entrusted with the publication in England of *The Keys of the Kingdom of Heaven* (1644), by John Cotton (1585–1692), showing his Congregationalist convictions.

By the middle of the 1620s, it was becoming increasingly difficult to exist in the Church of England as a Puritan. Charles I (1600–1649) became king in 1625 and supported William Laud (1573–1645). Laud had an impressive rise through academic and ecclesiastical ranks, landing as chancellor of Oxford University and archbishop of Canterbury, the highest office in the Church of England. He was Arminian, sacramental, episcopal, and a royalist, all anathema to the Puritans. He attacked the Reformed consensus in the church and narrowed the boundaries of conformity. He enforced strict adherence to the Book of Common Prayer, requiring the wearing of priestly clothes, bowing, and precise placement of the communion table, which the Puritans deemed superstitious. He used degrading punishments, cutting off the ears of those who refused to conform and branding the foreheads of undeterred Puritans with the letters "SL" for "seditious libeler." The Puritans made light of this by joking that the letters stood for *stigmata Laudis*, or the "sign of Laud." By the mid-1630s, suppression of criticism and nonconformity was severe, and the fallout was great. Goodwin resigned his positions in Cambridge in 1634 and fled to the Netherlands in 1639.

Goodwin returned and settled in London in 1641. The Long Parliament (1640–1648) had convened, and civil war broke out. Charles had assembled Parliament in 1640 because he needed money. He had exhausted his resources in the Bishops' Wars, his failed attempt to force Laudianism on Scotland. That Parliament had Puritan sympathies reveals both the effectiveness of the Puritans, even under persecution, and how unpopular Laud's zealous reforms really were. The Puritan Parliament went to war against the king and won in 1646. It tried and executed Laud in 1645 and then King Charles himself in 1649. During these tumultuous years, Goodwin served in the Westminster Assembly, the religious advisory body to Parliament, and was vocal about his congregationalist ecclesiology and other key theological topics.

Goodwin was close to Oliver Cromwell (1599–1658), the general of the parliamentary military and later Lord Protector, after Charles was executed and Parliament dismissed in 1653. Cromwell was a firm, efficient, and moderate Puritan, and he ruled during a time of religious toleration by the standards of the day, by which only Roman Catholicism and unorthodox sects were forbidden. Cromwell showed his favor to Goodwin with an appointment to the presidency of Magdalene College, Oxford. From this post he helped the school both academically and spiritually. This was the height of his political and ecclesiastical career. During this decade he served in numerous significant roles in the Cromwellian government and was part of the inner circle with John Owen (1616–1683) and Phillip Nye (1592–1672), who wrote the Savoy Declaration (1658), the Congregationalist revision of the Westminster Confession of Faith (1646). Goodwin's fate was tied to Cromwell and the Commonwealth, however, and when Oliver died in 1658 and his son, Richard Cromwell (1626–1712), failed to command the same influence as his father, the whole Puritan project unraveled. Goodwin left his position at Oxford and went to London, where he pastored an independent congregation.

The final decades of Goodwin's life were spent in relative obscurity compared with his high-profile career as part of the Westminster Assembly, chaplain to Cromwell, college administrator, and public political figure. He focused on his people as a pastor and on his writing ministry. This was the lot of many Puritan establishment figures after 1660, when the monarchy was restored and the remaining Puritan pastors lost their church positions. In many ways, the failure of Puritanism as a political movement in England and ecclesiastical movement within the Church of England forced these godly ministers to devote their energies toward that which they most excelled, namely pastoral ministry and pastoral theology.

THIS BOOK

At the outset, let me be clear about what this book is not. It is not a complete biography of Thomas Goodwin. Neither is it an exhaustive treatment of his doctrine of assurance. Nor is it my intention to enter into all of the nuanced debates surrounding the theme of assurance in the seventeenth century, or even to reference them. What I offer here are highlights from Goodwin's experience informed by analysis of the contours of his theology of assurance, with enough historical context to make sense of both, but ultimately aimed at the assurance of faith for Christians today.

We will look at the doctrine of assurance in the life and writings of Goodwin from six related angles, each corresponding to a period of his experience, and at the same time draw application for Christians and the church today along the way. I said at the beginning that all Christians desire assurance of faith and that all sincere believers also experience seasons of doubt. This certainly resonates in my own life, as one who has struggled with doubt on many occasions and sought relief through various means—prayer, confession, memorization of biblical promises, holiness, and more. Assurance has also proved to be one of the foremost pastoral care touchpoints in my pastoral ministry. People want to know they are going to heaven, myself included, and many simply are not certain, for a myriad of different reasons. My hope is that bringing Goodwin to bear on our contemporary striving for assurance will give insight to Christians in general about their own souls and equip pastors and local church leaders in the discipleship of their people. The Puritans wrestled with the doctrine and experience of assurance more than any other group in history, and Goodwin was a leader among his peers. Looking to him on the subject both critically and with appreciation, I believe, will be eminently helpful.

CHAPTER 1

The Struggle for Assurance

Thomas Goodwin grew up in a Christian home, and the Holy Spirit worked on his heart from a young age. Yet Goodwin would not come to a saving faith until his university days, after a season of rebellion precipitated by an embarrassing episode as a student. After surrendering to Christ, he struggled for years with doubt. Later in life, he reflected on both the causes of doubt and God's purposes in it, offering insights relevant to Christians today.

EARLY YEARS AND EDUCATION

Goodwin's conversion to Christ took place just three days prior to his twentieth birthday, yet as he recalled, his spiritual pilgrimage began with his birth into a pious family. It was in this family that he gained an early familiarity with the things of God and experienced the workings of his conscience. His conscience restrained him from gross immorality and even made him weep over his sins in conviction. From time to time when Goodwin contemplated God, he was filled with a sense of joy and peace. These urgings and inclinations of conscience away from sin and toward God stemmed merely from what Goodwin identifies as nature, or that which any person might experience by themselves when confronted with the truth of the gospel. Yet Goodwin convinced himself it was grace, and shortly after his becoming a student at Cambridge he participated in a communion service. It was Easter, and he was fourteen at the time. Given this was his first time receiving the sacrament, he diligently prepared his heart for the occasion. A kind of spiritual high was the result. He remembers, "After having received it, I felt my heart cheered after a wonderful manner, thinking myself sure of heaven, and judging all these workings to be infallible tokens of God's love to me, and of grace in me."[1] But God would not allow Goodwin to continue in his false sense of security. His much-anticipated next communion experience proved a grave disappointment.

Once again, Goodwin diligently prepared himself for the Lord's Supper celebration in chapel. He faithfully attended Richard Sibbes's sermons and devoured John Calvin's *Institutes of the Christian Religion*. Ready for the big day, seated in the chapel during the service, he received a message from his tutor, William Power, forbidding him to receive the sacrament. The sanction was based on Goodwin's young age and presumed immaturity, an assumption vindicated by Goodwin's response. Understandably embarrassed by the necessity of his exit in front of the whole college, he pitied himself for the humiliation and resented the missed opportunity at spiritual gratification. He gave up prayer and the study of sound theology, gave up listening to Puritan preaching by Sibbes and others, and instead devoted himself to acquiring eloquence and the ability to preach in the way that was applauded in the university and by educated society.

During his sojourn in self-promotion, Goodwin dabbled in Arminianism (a theology of salvation that emphasizes human choice), which was being hotly debated at the time in the Netherlands and, thanks to the Synod of Dordt (1617–1619), all over Europe and the British Isles. He also switched from Christ's College to Catherine Hall, Cambridge, likely to receive sooner advancement to fellow, a position to which he was quickly appointed. He found himself caught in a cycle of hypocrisy. Leading up to communion he would examine himself, repent, and turn to God, but once the sacrament was over, he would quickly slide back into prayerlessness and hardness of heart. At one point Goodwin was feeling depressed and ready to give up trying all together. During this period he found himself on route to a party with his old friends at Christ's College, when he was pressed by one of his companions to sit in on a funeral sermon. It was October 2, 1620, and everything changed.

CONVERSION

A sermon was the last thing Goodwin wanted to sit through. He really did not enjoy preaching in general, though he was studying divinity, and he especially disliked the dull stuff that was common around Puritan Cambridge at the time. But he saw eminent scholars filing in and so thought that it might be worth his time, and if it was not, he figured he could always pack up, leave, and spend time with friends that afternoon. The preacher was Thomas Bainbridge (d. 1646), the text was Luke 19:41–42, and Goodwin was cut to the heart. Bainbridge powerfully preached the danger of deferring repentance from Jesus' lament over Jerusalem and the fact that it was too late for his beloved city and people to avoid judgement. Exiting the church, Goodwin could no longer carry on with his plans and returned to Catherine Hall alone.

Goodwin was unable to control his thoughts at this point. He vividly remembered, "I thought myself to be as one struck down by a mighty power ... and I, endeavoring not to think the least thought of my sins, was passively held under the remembrance of them, and affected, so as I was rather passive all the while in it than active." His mind sensed the depths of his depravity, illuminated by the new light of Christ. This was not merely what the natural person would recognize as sin, but Goodwin's thoughts were drawn to all manner of lusts and twisted desires flowing from the fountain of ungodliness in his heart. For the first time, he truly comprehended the corruption of his fallen nature and the depth of his depravity resulting from original sin. This provided no excuse, however, for he said of Adam's sin, "I did on my own accord assume and take on me the guilt of that sin, as truly as any of my own actual sins."[2]

At this point, Goodwin began recollecting his life up to this climactic moment. How he experienced conviction in his early years. How his college years were marked by a cycle of false repentance and fake spiritual life leading up to communion. How when he was denied the sacrament he began intentionally living with ambition for glory and praise. All of this proved to him that he had not yet experienced true saving grace. In fact, it terrified him. He considered the wrath of God he deserved, the just sentence of hell as his punishment, and was painfully aware of his deadness in sin and total inability to change his condition and circumstance. God would have to intervene in the situation if Goodwin were to be converted.

The intervention came as two "whispers." Goodwin describes it this way: "God took me aside, and as it were privately said unto me, 'Do you now turn to me, and I will pardon all your sins though never so many, as I forgave and pardoned my servant Paul, and convert you unto me, as I did Mr. Price, who was the

most famous convert and example of religion in Cambridge.'"
He explains that the example of Paul was pertinent because it
showed both the amplitude and the possibility of his pardon,
Paul being a persecutor of the church. This brought relief from
the intense conviction he was under. As for Price, he was the
most holy man Goodwin knew, and the promise of a new heart
like his brought great hope. Goodwin adamantly insisted that
these suggestions came immediately from God. They were perfectly timed, true when evaluated by God's word, and effectual,
for Goodwin experienced conversion, a heart change inexplicable apart from divine grace. He went from being inclined
toward sin to pulled toward the heart of God. This resulted in
true godliness in his life. The evidence of grace Goodwin iden-
tified included a complete shift to plain-style Puritan preaching
and the abandonment of seeking church promotions. But what
he beautifully identifies as "the most eminent property of my
conversion" was that "the glory of the great God was set up in
my heart as the square and rule of each and every particular
practice, both of faith and godliness, that I turned unto."[3]

QUEST FOR ASSURANCE

Despite his newfound faith, Goodwin spent the years following his conversion in a struggle for assurance, joy, and peace in
believing. Later in life he recalled, "I was diverted from Christ
for several years, to search only into the signs of grace in me.
It was almost seven years ere I was taken off to live by faith on
Christ, and God's free love, which are alike the object of faith."
His son claimed to have more than one hundred sheets of his
father's diary from the period full of observations about the pos-
ture of his heart and mind toward God and evaluations of his
progress in holiness. Goodwin recounts of those years, "I was
pitched on this great principle, that if I found I was sanctified,

as I plainly did, I then was certainly justified. ... I pursued after mortification of lust, and of holiness within, and then I thought I should have the comfort of justification, or of being justified."[4]

Price, whom God brought to Goodwin's mind at the moment of his conversion, became a close friend and confidant and offered counsel during Goodwin's struggle to rest in Christ. He encouraged him with the fact that trials of all kinds are tokens of the Christian being in Christ and are driving the Christian to God. He reminded him that God knows the best time to fill his children with his love and provide a fuller sight of Christ's blessed presence. In the meantime, it is for his adopted sons and daughters to live by faith and in anticipation of this blessing, either in this life or the life to come. Price reaffirmed for his friend the truth that at times the "old man" referenced in Romans 7 reasserts himself in startling ways and that such points are opportunities to loathe him and long after Christ and his righteousness. But, alas, Goodwin continued to doubt. He described his doubt as "darkness," from Isaiah 50:10–11, which he translated,

> Who is among you that fears the Lord, that obeyed the voice of his servant, that walks in darkness, and has no light? Let him trust in the name of the Lord, and stay upon his God. Behold, all you that kindle a fire, that compass yourselves about with sparks; walk in the light of your fire, and in the sparks that you have kindled. This you shall have of my hand; you shall lie down in sorrow.[5]

Such darkness is soul crushing. The only thing that could be worse would be losing the favor of God eternally. The darkness is distress of conscience from a feeling of being deserted by God. It is a total lack of assurance of salvation. True believers may experience seasons of darkness that last days, even years. This concept has made it into Christian parlance as the "dark night of the soul."[6] Principally, this darkness should be understood as "the want of inward comfort in their spirits, from something that is between God and them; and so meant of that darkness and terrors which accompany the want of the sense of God's favor." Goodwin adds, "And so darkness is elsewhere taken for inward affliction of spirit and mind, and want of light, in point of assurance, that God is a man's God, and of the pardon of a man's sins."[7] This darkness is an acute cause of misery and distress. Uncertainty about one's relationship with God and eternal state is incapacitating precisely because it is all-consuming.

The particulars of this internal distress are described by two phrases in the Isaiah passage: "having no light" and "walking in darkness." The absence of light makes the testimony of God's grace impossible to see. There is no immediate witness of the Spirit, what Goodwin refers to as the Spirit's sealing. There is no comfort from manifest graces in one's life, with no light to see them by. Even the memory of past graces or seasons of confidence fades for lack of illumination. When one walks in darkness, there is hesitation about direction, whether one is destined for heaven or hell. When one walks in darkness, there is the tendency to stumble over everything, even the promises of God in Scripture only discourage. The darkness fills one with terror and horror. As children see fearful sights in the dark, the doubting Christian sees God's impending wrath as an enemy.

Goodwin was not unique in his doubt. He later argues that many believers lack assurance of their salvation. The "full assurance of faith" referenced in Hebrews 10:22, for instance, is an assurance that one is accepted by God, that one's sins have been atoned for by the blood of Christ. But just as many do not have "hearts sprinkled clean from an evil conscience," as the second half of the verse states, that is, hearts that do not condemn, it is not uncommon for believers to lack full assurance. Regardless, those with weak faith are still called to come to God in prayer through Christ. The exhortation from the writer of Hebrews describes how one should ideally draw near to God, namely, with a pure conscience, but as is the case with most exhortations, the author is not insisting on a minimum standard.[8] What Goodwin found in Hebrews was not isolated biblical support for the idea that true believers could and probably would lack assurance. Psalms 42–43 describe one whose soul is downcast, whose hope is God alone, despite circumstances and feelings to the contrary.

That Christians find themselves doubting their standing before God is possible because faith and assurance, at least full assurance, are distinct. Paul asks the Galatian Christians a rhetorical question, "Who has bewitched you?" (Gal 3:1), because they have been deluded by Satan about the very doctrine of justification. Jewish teachers came peddling the idea that a man had to become a Jew—namely, be circumcised—in order to be a true follower of Jesus. This adds up to justification by works, and Paul is infuriated that this false teaching has taken hold. Justification is being declared righteous before God based on the imputed righteousness of Christ, which is appropriated by faith alone. The Galatians were tricked into believing that there were prerequisites to justification. That the grace of justification must be earned.

In Goodwin's mind, if true believers can be misled about the doctrine of justification, "How much more may they, and ordinarily they are, misled in the application of faith, in the believing their own personal justification."[9] Goodwin's point is this: it is easier to be misled about one's appropriation of justification by faith than the doctrine itself, and yet the whole church in Galatia seems to have the latter mixed up. This confusion is one step further than questioning the reality of one's personal justification. Not only is it possible to doubt, but it is the ordinary Christian experience.

THE CAUSES OF DOUBT

In Goodwin's understanding, there were three potential causes of doubt: the Spirit of God, the guilty and fearful heart, and Satan. First, the Holy Spirit may be an agent in this distress of doubt. He at times stops witnessing our adoption, stops his positive testimony regarding our personal salvation in Christ. Instead, he may make impressions of God's wrath toward former sins, bringing the past to mind. He does this when provoked with presumptuous sins and the willful disobedience of the Christian. In response the Spirit may "shake over him the rod of his eternal wrath," hurling hypothetical and conditional threats.[10] Satan and our hearts increase this darkness with false conclusions. The Spirit's operation is holy, righteous, and true, but the flesh and the devil take advantage of it to bring "false and fearful conclusions" to the consciences of believers. Goodwin writes,

> They start amazing doubts and fear of their utter want of grace, and lying under the curse and threatenings of eternal wrath at the present, yea, and further, of eternal rejection for the future, and that God will never be merciful; and so lay them lower, and cast them into further darkness and bondage than the Holy Ghost was cause of, or intended; misinterpreting and perverting all these his righteous proceedings, as interpreting that withdrawing his light and presence, and hiding himself, to be a casting them off, so, likewise, misconstruing that temporary wrath, chastising and wounding their spirits for the present, to be no other than the impressions and earnest of God's eternal vengeance; and arguing, from their being under wrath, themselves to be children of wrath; and misapplying the application of all those threatenings of eternal damnation made by the Spirit, but in relation

and under a condition of such and such courses for the future, to be absolute against their persons, and to speak their present estate.[11]

The Christian who doubts believes these lies because of the temporary faith in others. That seed that falls on rocky, shallow soil (Matt 13:20–21) is mistaken for sincere, regenerating faith. In a positive light, it is this tendency that the writer of Hebrews picks up on in order to motivate perseverance (Heb 6:4–6). But negatively, observing those who appear to fall away may fuel anxiety about the possibility of one's own eternal demise.

Apart from our hearts piling on to the Spirit's operation, they can also deceive us. This should come as no surprise. We are naturally weak and defined by creaturely infirmity (Ps 103:14), even apart from our natural depravity derived from original sin. The natural mind is dark (Rom 1:19–23), what Goodwin describes as "carnal reason," which is opposed to faith.[12] Carnal reason inflates our estimation of ourselves before salvation and then, after regeneration, causes us to think too little ourselves despite our new identity in Christ. Carnal reason recruits other corrupt affections as well. Self-love, for example, tends toward self-flattery in the unbeliever, but the other side of this may be suspicion and skepticism in the life of the Christian. Carnal reason and genuine guilt, added to our natural state of weakness, mean doubt will surely be our experience apart from the active work of the Holy Spirit.

Goodwin's analysis proves most insightful in his tracing of Satan's role in robbing the believer of assurance. The devil has "a special inclination, and a more peculiar malicious desire, to vex and molest the saints with these sorts of temptations, of doubts and disquietness that God is not their God; so as all his other temptations unto sin, are but the laying in and barreling up the gunpowder, and making of the train, for the great plot of blowing up all."[13] Why is Satan so singularly intent on destroying assurance of faith? Above all the graces of God, he is most opposed to faith. As the archenemy of God, he delights to blaspheme the work of the Holy Spirit. He envies allegiance to God that once belonged to him, and doubting our salvation in essence accuses God of being a liar. Satan whispers doubts in our ear frequently and relentlessly, bringing a multitude of considerations at once, distracting our attention away from comforting truths and turning our mind to false conclusions and their accompanying terror. In the lives of those with saving faith, Satan's primary objective is to sow doubt.

Satan works on carnal reason, the guilty conscience, as well as our emotions, to corrupt our affections. In his attacks, he has the upper hand, for Satan, as "the tempter" and "the accuser," has been a student of humanity night and day since the fall of Adam and Eve, honing his craft and getting better. As a result, he knows precisely how and when to deliver his false reasoning. He has been taking notes and has various strategies depending on the personality, temperament, position, experience, spiritual maturity, and situation of his target. For instance, he may take advantage of the different ways God saves. Some have a clear, decisive, definite salvation experience that is marked by light following darkness, while others slowly grow in the knowledge of God and holiness. Satan will suggest that those who do not have the singular, defining experience ought not to be so confident about their saving faith. He communicates these lines of thinking in such a way that it is impossible to discern that it is him, therefore deceiving believers and stealing their assurance.

Satan also operates on our guilty consciences. Such operation consists of what Goodwin terms "false majors" and "false minors," which he compares to the two wings of an army. False majors are misunderstandings of how God works his grace or the truth of Scripture. For example, the idea that relapsing into the same sin again and again is incompatible with grace grants Satan a ready weapon in his attack on assurance. False minors, on the other hand, are accusations against us individually, playing on the guilt already present in our own hearts. These may hit their mark despite a biblical understanding of grace and a proper interpretation of Scripture. The devil's logic is syllogistic, the major premise being "those in whom any sin reigns, or in whose hearts hypocrisy and self-love is the predominant principle, are not in the state of grace." The minor premise, then, is "but such a one are you."[14] The conclusion inevitably follows that one is not saved. The major premise is indisputably true. It is in the minor premise that Satan works his deception. He will bring up a multitude of sins, a host of duties neglected, and the wicked desires of the heart. But the assumption that this infers the minor premise, that sin reigns and we are hypocrites, that we are not saved, is utterly false. The evidence that we continue in sin, sins of both commission and omission, of course, is overwhelming, but that sin reigns and hypocrisy predominates is objectively false for those who are in Christ.

The whole discussion about Satan being the slanderer and accuser raises an interesting question. Where does he get the seemingly inexhaustible evidence for his charges against us? Goodwin is quick to caution that only God can search and know the heart and the conscience. Yet Satan seems to know all. Generally speaking, he knows what corrupt hearts usually produce, and he is particularly savvy at drawing from this. In particular, however, demons are rational creatures that make it their business to study men and women personally and learn and discern their actions (Job 1:8–11). They listen to vocal confession of sin, whether in private or public prayer. They listen when we ask a brother or sister for accountability in overcoming a certain sin. They witness all we do, "being with us at bed, board, and in all company."[15] From all of these outward observations they are able to accurately guess our inner corruptions. A man who gratifies his flesh with pornography in secret will likely fall to temptation when presented with adultery because of the underlying heart problem of lust. But up to this point, the advantages demons, or angels in general, have over one man watching another remain a matter of degree. They have been studying people for millennia and never have to rest like us corporeal creatures. For Goodwin, however, there is more.

Here Goodwin gets technical in his discussion of how angels may know and manipulate the imagination and emotions, while the true thoughts and intentions of an individual's heart are only accessible to God. The angels' insight and operation takes place in the spheres of fantasy, or the faculty of imagining things, and the interchange between passion and bodily function. Our understanding, thinking, and reasoning are echoed in our imagination and catalogued in our subconscious. While the two—thoughts and the capacity to imagine—are intimately linked, they are also distinct. And while angels cannot access the former, they can know and operate in the realm of the latter. This is why they can impose thoughts and inner temptations. This explains both diabolical and angelic dreams, which are many in Scripture. All our perceptions enter our fantasy and can be conjured by demons unto our temptation or marshaled by angels for our help. Further, because reason pulls from the content of the fantasy or imagination, which angels have access to, when we are thinking or musing, they can judge what is on our mind.

Angels can also discern and influence our emotions, what Goodwin terms "passions." This results from their ability to know and "to move and stir those spirits and humors," what we today might call feelings and chemicals, "electively, wherein these passions are seated."[16] Our emotions and biology cannot be neatly separated. The will is tied to our desires and affections in a reciprocal relationship. We want, we act, we feel, we want, we act, and so on, and both our desires and emotions are accompanied by corresponding physical responses. Some of these are quite observable. Fear paints the face white, and shame makes it flush. Acute moments of anxiety can be as debilitating as a heart attack. But all passions are tied to some movement in the body. While angels do not have direct access to the will, they very much do have access to the integrated visceral dimensions of our emotions. Consequently, they know how we are feeling and can even stir our emotions by working on our feelings and the chemical balances inside our bodies.

Satan can strike with the fear of doubt in other ways as well. After all, Scripture describes him as a roaring lion on the prowl. Again, by way of caution, only God can wound the conscience directly and make an impression of his wrath on it. That said, "when the Holy Ghost has lashed and whipped the conscience, and made it tender once and fetched off the skin, Satan then may fret it more and more, and be still rubbing upon the sore, by his horrid suggestions and false fears cast in." Goodwin adds more vivid imagery: "He can, by renewing the experimental remembrance of those lashes which the soul has had from the Spirit, amaze the soul with fears of an infinitely sorer vengeance yet to come, and flash representations of hell-fire in their conscience … in such a manner as to wilder the soul into vast and unthought horrors." And on top of this, he can "bring home all the threatenings that are thundered forth in the word against hypocrites and men unregenerate, and discharge them all with much violence and noise upon a poor doubting soul."[17] Against such an adversary one might be tempted to despair, but the enemy is bound by the permissive will of God. The question then becomes, Why would God allow his children to experience such painful doubt?

THE PURPOSE OF DOUBT

There are three extraordinary instances found in Scripture of God leaving his own in the darkness of doubt. One can be explained only as God's prerogative. Just as Jesus said the man born blind was afflicted for the glory of God, there are times when God allows darkness in our lives for inscrutable reasons. Take Job as an example. His suffering went from physical loss to the spiritual woe of doubting his favor with God. Yet there is no explanation as to why God granted Satan permission to strike his servant. In fact, when Job questions God in his agony he is quickly put in his place by the sovereign of the universe, who makes clear that he is not beholden to Job. Suffering doubt can make one eminently wise and able to comfort others, for "who are they who are furnished with such apt, and fit, and seasonable considerations to comfort such, but those who have had the same temptations, and have been in the like distresses?"[18] Finally, in the case of an abundance of comfort and revelations, God will at times leave the believer in the darkness of doubt. The rule of 2 Corinthians 1:5 holds true, namely, that great sufferings and great comfort go hand in hand.

But beyond such extraordinary cases, there are ordinary cases in which doubt often reigns in the Christian. When guilty of self-confidence, doubt often strikes. This confidence can stem from trusting too much in true signs of grace, especially in the past, such as a conversion experience or season of tremendous victory over sin. It can flow from thinking that true signs of grace are somehow rooted in us rather than God in Christ. When the gifts of prayer, Christian fellowship, and the ordinances are neglected, assurance naturally wanes. When there is neglect in our hearts, such that these means of grace become merely ritualistic, certainty diminishes. In the case of gross sin, or the presence of any sin marked by refusal to confess and repent, for that matter, formal church discipline casts doubt on the state of the soul. When unmoved by God's chastisement through outward affliction, this stubbornness may result in the loss of assurance. When deserting the truth in the face of persecution, for instance, or refusing to profess it, as Jonah did, doubting ensues. Goodwin writes, "As when we are ashamed of Christ, the punishment fitted to it is, that Christ will be ashamed of us, so when we will not witness for God, there is no reason his Spirit should witness to us."[19] The case may even be that in the experience of the joy of assurance, we become ungrateful and view the grace and assurance of God as common. Whatever the case, be it extraordinary or ordinary, God works his purposes in doubt.

Goodwin offers a number of possible ends for which God may leave his own children in the affliction of doubt. These goals center on either God and his faithfulness or the increase of graces and destruction of corruption in the life of the believer. God may leave the believer in darkness simply to show his power and faithfulness in healing a wounded spirit. He may do it to show the power of Christ's resurrection through the fellowship of his sufferings. After all, Christ had to persevere through the darkness of Gethsemane and abandonment at the cross. God may allow doubt to more clearly manifest the difference between earthly life and the joys of heaven. We walk now by faith and not by sight (2 Cor 5:7). Or he may be simply reminding the doubter where spiritual comforts come from. The experience of intense doubt can be the means of discovering more fully the grace of faith. Faith proves itself when "a man relies on God, when all his dealings would argue he had forsaken a man, that though God put on never so angry a countenance, look never so sternly, yet faith is not dashed out of countenance, but can read love in his angry looks, and trust God beyond what he sees." The darkness of doubt can further be a means to destroy the flesh, to humble, to motivate obedience and the fear of God, to drive to prayer, and to cause the believer "to prize the light of God's countenance."[20] In every season of doubt, the believer may be confident of God's purpose, even if not assured in their faith.

FOR TODAY

Christians today are no less fallen and embattled with a sin nature than Goodwin and his contemporaries. Satan is still on the prowl. In fact, to Goodwin's point about the devil honing his craft, Satan has only improved his powers of accusation and slander over the past four hundred years. Alas, Christians in the twenty-first-century West are as plagued by doubt as ever. Moreover, three of Goodwin's causes of doubt, or situations in which it thrives, are particularly rife within evangelicalism.

Lack of Church Discipline

Few things rob the believer of assurance like ongoing sin. Yet few churches practice biblical church discipline as outlined by Jesus in Matthew 18. It is a failure at every level. Most do not emphasize church membership enough to make accountability possible. How can a church confront sin or sanction someone when no prior commitment or submission to such authority was made by the individual? When formal membership does exist, how often do brothers and sisters in Christ go to one another individually and rebuke sin? Gossip is not addressed; at best the inappropriate information simply goes no further. Overindulgence is not challenged; often the ability is coveted. Because sin is not attended to on a personal level, the discipline process almost never moves to the second stage, which is taking two or three others to speak with the individual. Taking the final action of telling the whole church, followed by excommunication or disfellowshipping, only happens when it is particularly gross or visible sin, something like a debilitating addiction or adultery. When it does happen, everyone cringes, questioning the prudence of calling into question someone's personal relationship with Jesus, but these are the keys of the kingdom given by Jesus and intended for the flourishing of the church. The aim of the church discipline process is restoration, not revenge. However, the success rate is incredibly low because of the plethora of church options and the refusal to follow up with previous churches when a newcomer shows up. The result? Church hopping and sin in the lives of believers, deflating the assurance of faith.

Refusal to Profess the Truth

Goodwin makes the observation that when Christians deny Christ, they often wonder whether they were Christians at all. This could look like denial under torture or the threat of death. It could look like Jonah's obstinate refusal to tell the Ninevites God's message of destruction and the seeming abandonment of God he experienced in the belly of a great fish. But most often, at least in our context, refusal to profess the truth simply means not telling someone about Jesus or what he stands for when the opportunity arises. There are a whole host of reasons and justifications for this: we don't want to impose, rock the boat, call into question someone's sincerity, offend, not be able to answer follow-up questions, or look silly. Sometimes we just don't want to be inconvenienced. Most of the time we are just plain scared. This temptation to keep silent will only be compounded as the culture becomes increasingly hostile to Christian discourse, both in terms of theology and morality. As Goodwin potently puts it, if we will not witness for God, how can we expect that the Holy Spirit will witness to us that we are true sons and daughters of God? Our salvation doesn't depend on evangelism, but our assurance of salvation very well may.

Reliance on Past Experience

Evangelicals are right to emphasize the new birth. After all, Jesus says one must be born again. Regeneration remains the only entrance into heaven. But there exists an overemphasis on the experience of conversion as a singular, unmistakable event marked by crisis. The fallout of this goes both ways. There are some who are not aware of a time in their life when they did not trust Jesus. As a result, they doubt. The question, of course, is not whether there was a time when we did not trust Christ, but are we trusting Christ now? On the flip side, many look back on an acute experience of conversion and derive their assurance from it. This gets far less attention but is far more prevalent. It happens all the time. One will recall an intense period of conviction followed by an overwhelming sense of peace and joy after trusting Christ alone for salvation, and one begins to rest in that conversion experience, perhaps also coasting spiritually or even justifying sin. Again, the question is not whether we trusted Christ then, but are we trusting Christ now? In such situations God often uses doubt to drive the believer's gaze to Christ, rather than a fixation on an experience of the past or lack thereof.

This is the great hope for the Christian drowning in doubt, that God has purposes in seasons of uncertainty that he is surely accomplishing. Our doubt may be his merciful means of destroying the flesh, humbling us, motivating obedience and the fear of God, or driving us to prayer. His reasons may or may not be revealed in this life, yet they are manifold. Like a good shepherd, the Lord only leads his sheep through the valley of the shadow of doubt to arrive at greener pastures. He is always with them, even in the darkness.

CHAPTER 2

The Experience of Assurance

G oodwin began preaching at Trinity Church in Cambridge in 1628, serving as lecturer. He held this post until 1634, when conformity to the ecclesiastical demands became too much for his conscience to bear. Goodwin was a Puritan, after all, and the particulars of the Book of Common Prayer were increasingly being enforced by bishops of the Church of England at the behest of King Charles's archbishop of Canterbury, the notorious William Laud. Leaving his university positions was difficult. He later recalled, "it was the power of God alone that prevailed to make me do it. It was he alone made me willing to live in the meanest and most afflicted condition, so that I might serve him in all godly sincerity. I cheerfully parted with all for Christ, and he has made me abundant compensation, not only in the comforts and joys of his love, which are beyond comparison above all other things, but even in this world."[1]

Little is known about the next few years of Goodwin's life, but the Lord did provide, specifically in the form of Elizabeth Prescott, whom he married in 1638. He moved to Holland to escape persecution and pastored the English church in Arn-heim. It was just before these life-changing events that Good-win's seven-year struggle for assurance finally ended.

BLESSED ASSURANCE

The gospel advice that Price gave, which the Lord used to bring peace to Goodwin's conscience, was to look ultimately not to his sanctification but to the free grace of God in Christ for salvation. In the end, free grace and signs of grace go together in the life of the believer, working hand in hand to bring the assurance of faith. In Price's words to Goodwin,

> Yet this you may have remaining ever unto you, as an evidence of God's everlasting love, that the marks of true chosen ones are imprinted upon you, and truly wrought within you; for your eyes are opened to see yourself utterly lost; your heart is touched with a sense and feeling of your need of Christ, which is poverty of spirit; you hunger and thirst after Christ and his righ-teousness above all things; and it is the practice of your inward man to groan and sigh, to ask and seek for rec-onciliation with God in Christ. These things you have to comfort you against sin and Satan, and all the doubts of your own heart. Therefore, when you fear that all is but hypocrisy, to fear is good and wholesome, but to think so is from the flesh, carnal reason, Satan, dark-ness, because it is against that truth which has taken place in your heart, merely of God's free favor towards you in Jesus Christ.[2]

In other words, evidence of grace in one's life can be a comfort, but the foundation of assurance is God's forgiveness in Christ. Sage, Puritan advice indeed.

Goodwin responded to his friend with joy, "I am come to this pass now, that signs will do me no good alone; I have trusted too much to habitual grace for assurance of justification. I tell you Christ is worth all."[3] He later recounted that the line of thinking that finally brought comfort was the covenant of grace. Just as there were two branches of original sin, namely, the imputation of Adam's guilt and the corruption of human nature, so there were two elements of being in Christ rather than Adam. With the headship of Christ comes the imputation of his righteousness for justification and a holy nature derived from him for sanctification. The enlightening conclusion for Goodwin was that, while Christ's righteousness for justification was perfect, his own sanctification would be imperfect until glorification. While justification and sanctification are certainly related, they must not be confused. When one infringes on the other, an early casualty is always assurance.

For Goodwin, however, finding assurance is more than simply forming a correct understanding of theology; it is also a work of the Spirit. We will get to Goodwin's theology of the sealing of the Spirit in the next chapter, but he believes the Spirit's work to be twofold. The Holy Spirit operates on the mind, such that "a man knows his estate in grace, his understanding is fully convinced of it," and at the same time "the will and affections do taste the sweetness of it beforehand." Goodwin reflects, "There is nothing sweeter than the love of God, and the tasting of that sweetness is the earnest of the inheritance." The Spirit's assurance is a "taste of heaven." The apostle Peter describes it as "joy unspeakable and full of glory" (1 Pet 1:8, Goodwin's translation). He is called the "Spirit of promise" (Eph 1:13, Goodwin's translation), because "he brings home the promise to a man's heart and assures him of an interest," an interest in the atoning sacrifice of Christ, that Christ was indeed the substitute for the individual personally. Goodwin likens this second work of the Spirit to his first work of regeneration. He writes, "It is a new conversion, it will make a man differ from himself in what he was before in that manner almost as conversion does before he was converted." This experience of the Holy Spirit as comforter can be compared to the heat of the sun on the earth and the change of seasons. One goes from the cold of doubt to the warmth of assurance, so "when the Holy Ghost comes in this manner upon the heart, it was winter before, but it will be spring."[4] These are just some of the ways Goodwin tries to capture the relief, freedom, and joy of the full assurance of faith.

TEN DIRECTIONS FOR ASSURANCE

For those who have not yet experienced this assurance, who are in the throes of doubt, Goodwin offers ten recommendations. They are cumulative tools that build on one another. First, do not make any hasty wishes or say things that will later cause regret. We find David doing this when he hastily claims that all men are liars, including Samuel and the promises he spoke from God (Ps 116:11), and again when he brashly says he is cut off from God (Ps 31:22). We do the same thing when we conclude that we will be cut off from God, swallowed up by Satan, and eternally destroyed, that previous graces were merely lies, falsehoods, or counterfeits. Or, like Job, we curse the day of our birth (Job 3:1–4), wishing we had never been born, or claim we would choose spiritual death over life (Job 7:15). Such ideas and statements might feel justified in the moment, but we will certainly regret them later, when the dust of grief and anger has settled. Moreover, God would deal more gently with us if it were not for our impatience. Just as a physician must deal more harshly with a patient who resists treatment, even to the point of violent restraint, so God must at times deal firmly with his children who refuse to be patient in their doubt. Doubt can be devastating, indeed, but that is no excuse to make accusations against God, which the devil will surely use against us in the future.

Second, Goodwin would tell the doubting Christian to search their heart diligently. What provoked God to hide himself? Is it a particular sin or maybe a particularly heinous sin? Goodwin believes that until such a sin is recognized, and the heart submits, there can be no true comfort. While not all doubt is caused by sin in the life of the believer, sin is often the culprit. It certainly is in the case of David after he takes Bathsheba and kills Uriah (Ps 51). Goodwin writes, "David easily knew what it was for which God broke his bones; for his very sin was the iron mace, the instrumental cause itself, of God's executing it upon him. The horror of that murder God used as the hammer to break him with, and as the rod to whip him with."[5] What is the chief cause of fear? Often it is bad theology or a device of Satan. In the case of the former, one must preach directly to oneself. This David does too, when he challenges, "Why are you cast down, O my soul, and why are you in turmoil within me? Hope in God; for I shall again praise him, my salvation and my God" (Ps 43:5). Mistaken thinking stems from faulty biblical interpretation, for instance, fearing one has committed the unpardonable sin of blaspheming against the Holy Spirit (Matt 12:31) or assuming that the warning of Hebrews 6:4 about those who fall from grace not being able to experience renewal means that such a case is a genuine possibility. Search diligently for the cause of doubt, because identifying the cause is part of the cure. Goodwin offers the astute advice to go to a wise spiritual counselor if the true cause of doubt continues to elude identification.

Third, Goodwin teaches we must be sure to give attention to what brings comfort. Do not be the person who is so consumed with doubt as to listen to comfort only in order to refute it. Goodwin describes such people as "in distress so filled with anguish and sense of misery, and so strongly prepossessed with desperate opinions, and so far put out of hopes, that they reject all that is spoken for their comfort." They study what God has done for them and in them in order to reason against it. They refuse comfort. "This sullen, peevish, desperate obstinance," Goodwin exhorts, "is a thing you ought to take heed of. For hereby you take Satan's part, and against those you ought to love so dearly, even your own souls."[6]

Goodwin's fourth direction is to remember how we formerly enjoyed our relationship with God. Just like one would pore over the legal documents and deed if the ownership of one's property were challenged, with an eye for proof of legitimacy, so should the child of God in the darkness of doubt scour the Scriptures and their own life for experiences of God's faithfulness in the past so they can trust him with the future. Look for a time when God spoke peace to your heart. Search for feelings in your past of genuine love you had for God. Was a promise ever fulfilled? The presence of a single promise indicates that all God's promises are operative, for every promise conveys the whole Christ. "Have you found a promise (which is a 'breast of consolation') milkless? Yet again suck; comfort may come in the end." Goodwin asserts of God's gracious dealings, "God remembers them to have mercy on you," and then asks, "Why should you not remember them to comfort you?"[7] Remembrance of a past assurance flowing from communion with God can help to restore the soul to such a condition again (Ps 77).

The fifth direction is to renew faith and repentance as if they had never existed before. Believe the gospel and repent of your sins as if it were the first time; after all, the Christian life does not just begin with these virtues but is continually sustained by them. Our perception may be that we are not in a state of grace, but no one is beyond grace who will put their trust in Christ and turn from their sin to God. One way or the other, repent and believe the gospel. A temptation when in the darkness of doubt can be to focus so much on what we lost that we forget to practice obedience anew. But when we do, it changes the game. It "baffles the devil exceedingly, and gets the advantage of him. For by this the suit is removed, all his old pleas dashed, this puts him upon a new reply, diverts the war, and indeed nonplusses him. For what can he say to it? He must now prove that you are incapable of grace, that you shall never repent, which all the world and devils in hell cannot prove."[8] When we are not sure about our salvation, we can always repent and believe afresh.

Sixth, Goodwin directs, rather than dispute, resolutely cast oneself on the mercy of God whether he saves you or damns you. This is Job's resolve. He cries, "Though he slay me, I will hope in him" (Job 13:15). What other option is there? As Goodwin puts it, "Say, Be I damned or saved, hypocrite or not hypocrite, I resolve to go on. And there is good reason for it. For if you should leave off to serve the Lord, and resolve never to look after him more, then you are sure to be damned."[9] Of course, resolving to believe, humbling oneself in repentance, praying, and attending to the means of grace will accompany no one to hell. Rather, herein lies the path of salvation. In fact, saving faith is just this, throwing ourselves on the mercy of God in Christ, owning our sin, and declaring that he would absolutely be just in sending us to hell for all eternity. That is what every son and daughter of Adam deserves, and no salvation exists apart from acknowledging this fact.

Seventh, Goodwin teaches to trust in the name of the Lord. The name of the Lord is a ground of confidence when there is nowhere else to turn. When one "resolves to fear God and obey him, the name of God is an all-sufficient prop and stay for his faith to rest on, when he sees nothing in himself, or in any promise in the world belonging to him."[10] The *name* of the Lord, in Goodwin's thinking, is packed with theological meaning. His name carries all of his attributes, especially his grace and mercy. His name is Jesus Christ, as he is righteousness to men and women. Goodwin defends these concepts biblically, pointing both to Exodus 34:6–7 and Jeremiah 23:6. In the Exodus passage, Yahweh declares his own name, "The LORD, the LORD, a God merciful and gracious, slow to anger, and abounding in steadfast love and faithfulness, keeping steadfast love for thousands, forgiving iniquity and transgression and sin, but who will by no means clear the guilty." Jeremiah, referencing Christ, says, "This is the name by which he will be called: 'The LORD is our righteousness.'" When in doubt, in a total absence of signs or evidence in us, we can still say God is our God because he is gracious and Christ brings righteousness.

Why is the name of the Lord alone a sufficient ground for faith to rest on? Goodwin helpfully answers this for us by offering us three reasons. First, the name of the Lord is an adequate prop for faith to rest on because the attributes of God and Christ's righteousness fully answer all wants, doubts, and objections we could ever have. Goodwin illustrates this at length. One beautiful passage leveraging Exodus 34:6–7 is worth quoting here.

> Are you in misery and great distress? He is merciful: "The Lord merciful." The *Lord*, therefore *able* to help you; and *merciful*, therefore *willing*. Yes, but you will say, I am unworthy. I have nothing in me to move him to it. Well, therefore, he is *gracious*. Now grace is to show mercy *freely*. Yes, but I have sinned against him long, for many years. If I had come in when I was young, mercy might have been shown to me. To this he says, "I am

long-suffering." Yes, but my sins every way abound in number, and it is impossible to reckon them up, and they abound in heinousness. I have committed the same sins again and again. I have been false to him, broke promise with him again and again. His name also answers this objection, he is *abundant in goodness*. He abounds more in grace than you in sinning. And though you have been false again and again to him, and broke all covenants, yet he is *abundant in truth*, also better than his word, for he cannot to our capacities express all that mercy that is in him for us. Yes, but I have committed great sins, aggravate with many and great circumstances, against knowledge, willfully, etc. He forgives *iniquity, transgression, and sin*, sins of all sorts. Yes, but there is mercy thus in him but for a few, and I may be none of the number. Yes, there is mercy for *thousands*, and he *keeps* it. Treasures of it lie by him, and are kept, if men would come and take them.[11]

A second reason that the Lord's name is sufficient for assurance stems from the fact that all the conditional promises made to us are yes and amen in Christ, for he has fulfilled the conditions on our behalf. The promises do not depend on graces in us precisely because Christ and his righteousness fulfills the requirements of the covenant undergirding our salvation. When we cannot rest on anything in us as an indicator of grace, it is proper to look to Christ as the fountainhead of all grace and hope. Finally, a third reason why the Lord's name grounds assurance is that everything God does is ultimately for his name's sake. What he does for us has nothing to do with anything in us, but only with what is in him. God's grace toward us springs from his love alone. God proved his love for us in Christ's death for sinners while we were still just that, sinners. Rest in the reality that God is merciful, that there is righteousness in his Son, and that he has directed us to trust in him. Rest here and "catch hold as on the horns of the altar. And if you die, die there."[12]

Eighth, Goodwin recommends waiting on God. Goodwin describes waiting as an act of faith but stretched out over time. Waiting is hope, with the expectation of help from God. It is an act of submission with contentment, should relief not come. And what is the alternative? From an eternal perspective, "indeed the escaping hell in the end is so great a mercy, that it is worth the waiting for all your days, though you endure a hell here, and get not a good look till the very last gasp and moment of living." But this waiting on the Lord is not a passive exercise. The means of comfort and recovery should be utilized diligently and constantly. The devil loves to make us doubt the efficacy of Scripture, prayer, the ordinances, and Christian fellowship. Our abandonment of the means of grace because they are seemingly doing no good is a great victory for our enemy. Goodwin cautions against trusting in the use of the means instead of God in the means, challenging, "Believe in God as if you used no means, and yet as diligently use the means, even as if your confidence were to be in them."[13] Wait on God, but wait actively.

Ninth, above all things, according to Goodwin, pray. Get others to pray, certainly, but the assurance of faith is communion with God. As with any intimate relationship, it must be developed privately. Plead with God for comfort. When sin and God's wrath meet in the conscience, lay open the soul and confess the sin, owning its consequences, and receive forgiveness. Goodwin vividly compares the relief of a soul poured out to the relief a sick individual experiences from vomiting. This is David's response when his soul is heaving in Psalm 51 after Nathan confronted him with his sin against Uriah and Bathsheba. Job describes the Lord as a fierce lion on the hunt, trying to put words to his feeling of abandonment (Job 10:16). From Goodwin's perspective, "Fall you down and humble yourself like a poor and silly lamb; if you die, die at his feet, mourning, bleeding out your soul in tears. ... Go and strip yourself, therefore, and with all submission present a naked back to him. And though every stroke fetches not blood only, but well-nigh your soul away, yet complain you not one whit of him. ... The higher he lifts his hand to strike, the lower let your soul fall down, and still kiss the rod when he is done."[14] In the darkness of doubt and the distress of conscience, we humble ourselves before God in prayer, as a dog inches toward the master that flogs him, seeking reconciliation. Only from this place of humility does a path forward present itself.

The next stage of pleading in prayer is something we might call biblical reasoning. We may beg God to remember his thinking toward us from eternity, his thoughts of peace and mercy. Or we may ask him whether he has forgotten his own character, which is gracious and abundant in kindness, or remind him that his Spirit is the Comforter. We may inquire about the purpose of his wrath. If it is victory over us, we are content to lay down our weapons and be conquered. If he aims at getting glory out of our eternal damnation, "tell him it is true, he may. And that this is some comfort to you, that he may have glory out of your death and destruction, who never yet had it out of your life. But yet desire him to consider this before he thrusts his sword into you, that he did first sheathe it in his Son's bowels, and that he may show as much power in overcoming his wrath as in venting of it. Yes, and have also greater glory thereby." Why greater glory out of salvation rather than damnation? Because we will never be able to satisfy his justice in hell, any more than the servant who owed ten thousand talents could pay up from debtors' prison, for "if satisfaction to his justice is his end, he might better accept that which his Son made him, and so he shall be sure to be no loser by you. And thereby not only receive the glory of his justice, but show the riches of his grace and mercy also, and so double the revenue of his glory in you."[15] The pleading and reasoning may continue on and on, until there is nothing else to say, at which point, simply groan, sigh, and sob, but pray.

Finally, Goodwin warns the doubter about settling for mere ease of conscience; rather, he encourages the desire for assurance of pardon and healing of one's relationship with God. In Goodwin's colorful fashion, he writes: "For God may slack the cords and take you off the rack when yet he has not pardoned you. A traitor who was cast into the dungeon, and had many irons on him, may be let out of the dungeon, and have his irons taken off, and have the liberty of the Tower, and walk abroad again, with his keeper with him, and yet not have his pardon."[16] Look for peace, not merely a truce. For pardon, not reprieve. A godly person's chief trouble is not the sting of sin, but the filth of the offense done to God. God's children don't merely fear his wrath but want his favor. This distinction between comfort and true assurance confronts us with a horrifying possibility—misguided confidence about our eternal destiny.

FALSE COMFORT

If it is possible for a child of light to walk in darkness, it is also possible for a child of darkness to walk in the light. Goodwin draws this concept from Isaiah 50:10-11, where the prophet writes, "Who among you fears the LORD and obeys the voice of his servant? Let him who walks in darkness and has no light trust in the name of the LORD and rely on his God," and then warns, "Behold, all you who kindle a fire, who equip yourselves with burning torches! Walk by the light of your fire, and by the torches that you have kindled! This you have from my hand: you shall lie down in torment." Jesus, picking up the same theme, teaches that "not everyone who says to me, 'Lord, Lord,' will enter into the kingdom of heaven," even after doing mighty works in Jesus' name (Matt 7:21). Clearly the dreadful circumstance of false assurance is possible, an experience of comfort and a clear conscience when one's future is hell. Two primary torches, to use Isaiah's metaphor, provide our own illegitimate light, bringing false relief to the darkness of doubt.

The first false torch by which a child of darkness may walk in light is believing in one's own natural righteousness. This natural righteousness Goodwin understands as "the common righteousness of civility and natural devotion," which can be found among both the heathen and those who have the benefit of being educated by biblical revelation. In the case of the latter, Jesus' parable of the soils proves instructive. Human hearts, "though they be stony unto God, yet *some sparks of fire* may be struck out of them by the word, by education, by enlightening of the conscience, and by the working upon self-love," yet in the final estimation these sparks are "those outward acts of righteousness which arise and spring from self-love and natural conscience, which die and remain not."[17] The crucial distinction is behavior modification versus heart change. The former we can do, and then misguidedly rest in our own righteousness. The latter only God can do, as it is the Holy Spirit's work of regeneration, at which point we rest in the righteousness of Christ alone.

The urgent question becomes how to identify the false comfort of self-righteousness, for which Goodwin provides some guidance. The origin of our own righteousness may be the influence of society, expectations of family, wisdom from the church, the desire to be perceived a certain way, or the like, whereas Christ's righteousness comes like fire from heaven, when the Holy Spirit burns up lusts, melts the heart, drives out the devil, and kindles sincere love for God and zeal for his glory. The fuel of our own righteousness is the last six of the Ten Commandments, those commands that deal with outward relationships, while the fuel of true righteousness includes the worship of God both public and private. Goodwin explains, "When men practice but so much righteousness as is necessary for them to do if they will live in the world in any comfort or credit, as to be just and sober is necessary, as also to frequent God's ordinances," this is but self-righteousness. But when one performs "such duties which the world regards not, as mourning for sin, taking pains with the heart in private, between God and a man's own soul, and feeds upon heavenly things and thoughts," added to these, "it is a sign it is more than common fire."[18] Goodwin continues in this vein, pitting contentment with the formal performance of duties with those done out of a heart warmed by heavenly fire. He reminds believers that there is a difference between motivation based on fear, whether fear of disgrace or hell, and motivation that springs from a genuine love for God and zeal for his glory. Again, motivation is a matter of the heart, which only the individual has access to and only God knows definitively.

The second false torch providing light to the child of darkness is the fire of physical comforts consumed by natural human desires. Goodwin makes much of this metaphor of light given off by fire. It is the creature comforts of houses, food, an attractive spouse, children, prestige, position, and the like that serve as the fuel for the fire. It is our lusts, set on the things of this world, which, while they are never satiated, consume what this world has to offer and give off a fake light. Many, while enjoying the pleasure and security this life may offer at times, "go on merrily, neglecting God and Christ, and communion with him."[19] But not so with the true believer. A true follower of Jesus will never be satisfied with outward comforts but will struggle until communion with God is restored. Only the enjoyment of him will satisfy an authentic Christian.

FOR TODAY

The logic of assurance presented by Goodwin—the possibility of assurance, the instructions for those in doubt, and the warning about false assurance—is universally instructive, as it is derived from Scripture and pastoral insight into common human experience. Grasping full assurance of faith continues to be a struggle for Christians in the twenty-first century. Those who have experienced the grace of God and are children of light may be walking in the darkness of doubt, but they are not doomed to this fate. The same Holy Spirit who comforted Goodwin's soul, a comfort accompanied by joy unspeakable, comforts those in Christ today. Whatever the cause of doubt may be, relief is possible, because nothing is impossible with God. This should provide comfort for those currently groping for assurance, as should Goodwin's ten practical directions for the doubting Christian.

Feelings

The actionable suggestions Goodwin gives to those who have lost their assurance and are longing to experience sweet communion with God are pure gold, not so much because the list is definitive, but because it is derived from a helpful principle of discipleship, namely, that feelings often follow obedience. Goodwin's ten instructions could be expanded, to be sure, and some readers may have genuine disagreements with individual directives depending on their underlying theological commitments. But Goodwin helpfully applies this essential principle of discipleship to the quest for assurance. So often in the Christian life we don't feel like walking in obedience. Our hearts are not motivated toward holiness, and our desire for sin can over-whelm our desire for holiness. Yet we must obey and trust that our feelings will follow. Every temptation to sin, whether infrac-tions of commission or omission, is at its root a crisis of faith. Do we believe that what God demands is not only right but best and will ultimately bring about our joy and fulfillment? If so, we proceed according to his will, even if we don't want to, and pray that our hearts will follow. The same goes for assurance. We wait on the Lord, as he alone can assure our hearts, but we are not passive in our patience. We avail ourselves of the means of grace—Scripture, prayer, biblical community—though they seem to be of no effect. We plead with God, though we sense no relationship with him. We remind ourselves of the promises found in Scripture, though they bring no immediate relief. We grasp what is true about our union with Christ, hoping for a renewed communion with him that alone can bring the comfort, peace, and rest of assurance.

False Assurance

Goodwin's warning about falsely derived assurance is potent, particularly regarding the fake assurance that can arise from the physical comforts of this world. Many Christians in modern society enjoy unprecedented safety, prosperity, and even respect, though the latter may be waning. Not long ago, church atten-dance and the label "Christian" brought social capital in many sectors. The pleasures this world has to offer, not bad in and of themselves, are readily available. Abundance and entertain-ment abound in seemingly ever-increasing amounts, standards of living improve, technology makes life more convenient and delivers what we want when we want it. Many in evangelical churches who would call themselves Christians and possess the ability to articulate the gospel and orthodox doctrine are content with consuming such comforts. The light put off by our physical desires being met is lulling some into the presumption that they are children of light, when in fact they are but children of darkness walking in a manufactured light. The specter of false assurance ought to drive those of us who call Jesus our Savior and Lord to evaluate whether we are assured of our faith because we are communing with God or consuming something less, which will end in eternal misery.

Goodwin experienced doubt acutely, but eventually his assurance was palpable and accompanied by indescribable joy. While there are certainly avenues the doubter might take to gain or regain confidence in salvation, the assurance of faith is not ultimately a change of mind. It doesn't flow from a change in behavior or harking back to assurance's memory. It is a work of the Holy Spirit. As we will see in the next chapter, Goodwin's theology of assurance, derived from both Scripture and his personal experience, was the pinnacle of a staple Puritan doctrine.

CHAPTER 3

The Theology of Assurance

Goodwin's doctrine of assurance did not appear in a vacuum. It was also informed by his experience. As we have seen, there was a significant period of time after he believed he was saved that he struggled with assurance. When assurance came, it brought with it a spiritual experience akin to conversion itself. Goodwin's understanding was also informed by doctrinal development in the wider Reformed tradition and contemporary Puritan discussions. In this chapter we will isolate the historical influences on Goodwin by briefly looking at assurance in the theologies of William Perkins (1558–1602), Richard Sibbes (1577–1635), and John Preston (1587–1628), and then the Westminster Confession of Faith's consolidation of the Puritan doctrine of assurance. This will lay the necessary groundwork for understanding Goodwin's exegetical and systematic treatment of the doctrine of assurance.

PURITANISM

As we will see, Goodwin equated the experience of full assurance with the sealing of the Spirit, and though this became popular later in the seventeenth century, it was a process of development, and the doctrine never became a universal consensus. John Calvin (1509–1564) actually taught the opposite. Assurance is included in faith, yet at the same time, there is no faith that is not tinged with doubt or at least potentially corruptible with doubt.[1] For Calvin, the Spirit is given as a seal to all Christians at conversion. It is impossible to believe without being sealed with the Spirit. Most crucially, the Holy Spirit himself is the seal. Sealing is not something the Spirit does.[2] The idea that the Spirit is the seal began to give way to sealing as an action of the Spirit in the understanding of the early Puritans.

A key representative of early Puritanism, especially on the doctrine of assurance, is William Perkins. Assurance preoccupied Perkins as his foremost pastoral problem. That God is utterly sovereign in salvation begs the question of how one can be certain one is among the elect. This, coupled with the general Puritan tendency to take sin and self-examination seriously, made assurance a frontline issue for Perkins. Perkins did not separate assurance from faith and make sanctification the ground of the former, but rather nuanced his understanding of assurance. There is both objective and subjective assurance. Objective assurance is included with faith as a confidence in the veracity of the promises of the gospel. Subjective assurance is realizing that those promises apply to us personally. The sealing of the Spirit became the Spirit's activity of working this subjective assurance in us. We become aware of our salvation both mentally and emotionally. We feel it. While the Spirit can witness to the reality of salvation directly, he does so most regularly by making the evidences of grace in our lives effective witnesses of our salvation. He draws our attention to the fruit of the Spirit in our lives, for instance, and assures us that it would not be present apart from him. Sanctification is an evidence of justification, but the foundation of assurance rests in Christ alone and our blood-bought union with him.[3]

Richard Sibbes, the one personally responsible for convincing Goodwin of the merits of plain-style preaching, spoke often on the sealing of the Spirit. He maintained Perkins's emphasis on sealing as an activity rather than the gift of the Spirit himself at conversion. He used the language of a "superadded work" and "work of the Spirit upon faith, assuring the soul of its estate in grace." This confirmation of saving faith is an internal work of the Spirit and not necessarily tied to the evidences of sanctification. He describes it in his characteristic, vivid language as joy, like a marriage to the perfect husband, Christ himself. The work is founded upon the very sealing of Christ by his Father with the Spirit, which for Christ was at his baptism.[4] As such, for Sibbes the sealing of the Spirit becomes the ultimate sign of grace in the life of the believer.

John Preston moved further along this trajectory and taught explicitly that the sealing of the Spirit was a second work of the Spirit in the lives of believers who attained a certain level of victory in their Christian walk. Sealing is totally illegitimate if not preceded by faith in Christ and holiness. We must first have enough evidence of grace, observable in our sanctification, to conclude that we are saved before we can hope for the Spirit's sealing and accompanying assurance, in Preston's estimation. In his own words, speaking of the believer, "When he has put to his seal, that God is true, then the Lord puts to his seal, and assures him that he has received him to mercy." This is a thing "we cannot express, it is a certain divine expression of light, a certain inexpressible assurance that we are the sons of God, a certain secret manifestation, that God has received us, and put away our sins. I say, it is such a thing that no man knows, but they that have it."[5]

As we shall see, this idea that sealing is a singular, spectacular work of the Spirit wrought only in some Christians, and accompanied by almost indescribable comfort and joy, is appropriated and developed by Goodwin.

WESTMINSTER

While Goodwin was part of this Perkins–Sibbes–Preston trajectory, the Westminster Confession of Faith, produced by the Westminster Assembly he participated in, reveals that his was not the only school of thought.[6] In fact, the Westminster Confession, like so many statements of faith, was a compromise document, one in which differing parties made concessions, especially on the issue of assurance, seeking to set the boundaries of the discussion rather than to definitively end the debate. Here are a few of the most relevant statements:

> Although hypocrites and other unregenerate men may vainly deceive themselves with false hopes … such as truly believe in the Lord Jesus, and love him in sincerity, endeavoring to walk in all good conscience before him, may, in this life, be certainly assured that they are in the state of grace.[7]
>
> This certainty is … an infallible assurance of faith, founded upon the divine truth of the promises of salvation, the inward evidence of those graces unto which these promises are made, the testimony of the Spirit of adoption witnessing with our spirits that we are the children of God: which Spirit is the earnest of our inheritance, whereby we are sealed to the day of redemption.[8]
>
> This infallible assurance does not so belong to the essence of faith, but … [the believer] may without

extraordinary revelation, in the right use of ordinary
means, attain thereunto.[9]

These statements clearly claim that assurance is possible, while
at the same time leaving it to pastors and Christians at large
to determine precisely *how* it is possible. This nuance is com-
plicated by the fact that false assurance is also clearly possible.
God's promises in Christ are the ground of assurance, which are
proven true in the life of the believer by both the evidences of
sanctification and the Spirit. Whether the Spirit's work is a separate, third category is unclear. Further, the sealing of the Spirit
is intentionally vague, as the Westminster divines knew full
well that the witness of the Spirit proved the hardest ground of
assurance to comprehend and therefore remained hotly debated.
All of this reveals that there were multiple opinions going into
the Westminster Assembly, which manifested themselves in
three approaches to assurance among those who could all, in
good conscience, subscribe to the Westminster Confession.[10]

The first approach was championed by Anthony Burges
(1600–1663), and taken up by representatives such as Jeremiah
Burroughs (1599–1646) and George Gillespie (1613–1648). For
these men, the witness of the Spirit must always be tied to the
witness of our spirits (Rom 8:15–16). The sealing of the Spirit
is not a separate experience, or a direct witness of the Spirit,
detached from the evidences of grace in the life of the believer.
Instead, the Spirit brings full assurance of faith through the
fruits of faith, namely, repentance and new obedience. These
concrete indicators protected against any smack of mysticism
or extra, special revelation regarding one's salvation, as well
as antinomianism that may result from assurance untethered
from holiness and sanctification. In brief, this approach pushed

Perkins's emphasis on the indirect witness of the Spirit, through evidence of faith, in the opposite direction from Sibbes and Preston, making it the exclusive mode of the Spirit's operation.

A second group of thinkers, including William Twisse (1578-1646), Samuel Rutherford (1600-1661), William Bridge (1600-1670), and Henry Scudder (1584-1659), believed that the Spirit could in fact witness directly to our spirits, assuring us that we are indeed sons and daughters of God. In contrast to the first group, for these men Romans 8:15 references a work of the Spirit that could be in addition to Romans 8:16. Confidence of salvation based on evidence is a deduction, as we reason that we are children of God. This reasoning is biblical and real as the Holy Spirit works through it to comfort us. It remains, however, an indirect witness. The Spirit may also go one step further and directly suggest the reality of adoption to the believer's soul. This approach follows Perkins and Sibbes in allowing for the Spirit's immediate testimony, while at the same time emphasizing the individual's reasoning from evidence of grace for full assurance. The believer can always look to signs of spiritual life and the pastor can observe them, making the deduction strategy practical, concrete, and more sheltered from abuse.

Finally, a third approach emerges with Goodwin and those influenced by him. While having affinity with the second group, as far as the two avenues for assurance go, this third scheme, far from precluding the immediate witness of the Spirit, emphasizes it as far superior to the evidence-based witness. Love for God's word and God's people may be fitting evidence of salvation but pales in comparison with the Spirit making us feel that salvation directly. The sealing of the Spirit is not merely an addition to deduction from evidence, nor is it a normal part of the Christian life. In fact, many believers never experience it at all. This understanding of assurance is a full flowering of the Perkins–Sibbes–Preston trajectory, complete with sealing as a second, immediate, singular work of the Spirit—so pronounced—that its impact is comparable to a second conversion.[11] This idea will become clearer as we look at Goodwin's exegesis and theology of assurance.

EXEGESIS: EPHESIANS 1:11–14

At the risk of being tedious, we need to walk through Goodwin's exposition of Ephesians 1:11-14. This is ground zero for his developed doctrine of assurance, with its emphasis on the sealing of the Spirit and his most sustained exegetical defense for his view. He translates the passage this way:

> In whom also we have obtained an inheritance, being predestined according to the purpose of him who works all things according to the counsel of his own will, that we should be to the praise of his glory, who first trusted Christ. In whom you also trusted, after you heard the word of truth, the gospel of your salvation. In whom also, after you believed, you were sealed with that Holy Spirit of promise, who is the earnest of our inheritance until (or, for) the redemption of the purchased possession, unto the praise of his glory.[12]

Goodwin splits the passage in half, verses 11-12 speaking of the Jews and the apostles and verses 13-14 of the gentiles, specifically the Ephesians in this instance. He is sensitive to context. The passage is an application of what came before in the previous ten verses, where Paul draws his readers into considering their blessings in Christ, in general God's acts of election, redemption, adoption, granting of a glorious inheritance, and bringing glory to himself through Christ. The text becomes personal in verse 11, as Paul applies what came before to Jewish believers for the purpose of comfort. They, Paul included, make up the "we." They have been effectually called, proven by the fact that the inheritance had been obtained. This calling follows the eternal decree of God in predestination. It is immutable, flowing from God's own purpose. All of this encouragement is founded on the fact that God works all things according to the counsel of his will, indicating that he is all-powerful and all-wise.

Verse 13 transitions from the application for the Jews, specifically the apostles, to the gentiles, particularly the Ephesians. The gentile Ephesians also trust in Christ and can experience the same confidence; they just have to hear "the word of truth," referred to as "the gospel of [their] salvation," as well. Goodwin explains from verses 13 and 14 that we as gentiles "have assurance of the love of God, and walk in communion with him. You, says he, are capable of having the same assurance, and we write to you these things, that you may have it; for the scope of that epistle is to beget assurance in the hearts of the godly."[13]

Armed with assurance as the primary theme of the book of Ephesians, Goodwin systematically lays out his understanding of the sealing of the Spirit from Ephesians 1:13–14. He articulates his doctrine in five points. First, he distinguishes the Spirit's sealing from faith. Some want to distinguish between the assurance of the truth of God's promises and the assurance of one's interest in those promises, coupling the sealing of the Spirit with the former. Goodwin agrees that assurance of the truth of God's promises is always present to some degree with faith, that it is a work of the Spirit, and that it can properly be called sealing. But this is not what Paul has in view in Ephesians 1. For one thing, the sealing is of people, not of promises or their validity. For another, this sealing is said to come after believing. Others will distinguish sealing from faith, but equate it with regeneration, sanctification, and renewal. Goodwin concedes that the stamping of the image of God on the heart is part of the Spirit's sealing, but that is not Paul's primary point. Paul clearly has in mind the assurance of an inheritance that is to come. If sealing is not faith, however, what is it?

Goodwin maintains that sealing is a metaphorical expression, or similitude, for a work of the Spirit. It is a *work* of the Spirit. Even though the Spirit himself is referred to as an earnest, a token, a pledge, or a down payment of our inheritance, saying he is a seal implies that he seals something or takes action on the human soul. The Holy Spirit is like a seal, though only a certain kind of seal may be appropriately imported into the simile. The work is not like that of a merchant who might place his seal on goods to distinguish them from others, like branding. Neither is it a security, guaranteeing significantly more in the future. It is the sealing of an inheritance that has already been made sure in Christ's finished work. In Goodwin's own words, "The principal scope of the holy Ghost here, [is] this, that they are sealed by the Spirit *to make them sure*, to make their persons sure of their salvation, to persuade their hearts, to put them out of question that this inheritance was theirs, that they might be able to claim it."[14] When the Holy Spirit seals us, he *does not make our salvation sure*, because this was decreed by God in eternity past and accomplished by the Son in time, but *he rather makes us sure of it*.

The sealing of the Spirit brings assurance of a particular kind. Goodwin distinguishes between two categories of assurance, a distinction crucial in Puritan theology. There is, first, "an assurance by sense, by conditional promises, whereby a man, seeing the image of God upon his heart, to which promises are made, comes comfortably to believe that he is in the estate of grace." Second, "there is an immediate assurance of the Holy Ghost, by a heavenly and divine light, of a divine authority, which the Holy Ghost sheds in a man's heart (not having any relation to grace wrought, or anything in a man's self), whereby he seals him up to the day of redemption." One is based on evidence; the other comes from the witness of the Spirit directly. It is intuitive, a "light that comes and overpowers a man's soul, and assures him that God is his, and he is God's, and that God loves him from everlasting." This total assurance is the comfort associated with the sealing ministry of the Spirit, and Goodwin defends this at length. To drive the point home, he concludes, "It is the electing love of God brought home to the soul; therefore, as election looks not to works nor graces, when God chose you to be his, so when he seals you up, the impress of that love is his without the consideration of works. A man does no know that he is God's by marks and signs, but by an immediate impress and light of the Holy Ghost's."[15] The assurance Goodwin has in mind is beyond reason and evidence, which can always be questioned. It is an experience that cannot be undermined by humankind, precisely because it is of God.

The second point Goodwin makes about sealing is the order. Sealing happens after saving belief, an assertion he defends both biblically and logically. From Scripture, Goodwin makes much of the example of the apostles, without giving attention to their unique location in redemptive history. According to his interpretation, these men were believers, trusting God by faith, before they were assured and given the seal of the Spirit. John 14, the heart of Jesus' discourse concerning the Comforter, makes clear that the disciples had faith and the Holy Spirit before they experienced the assurance of his sealing. Also, in Acts 15:7-9, in Peter's remarks to the Jerusalem Council, he speaks of the gentiles who already believed being given the Holy Spirit. Logically speaking, "Jesus Christ must first be mine, before I can say he is mine, the thing must be first; now he is made mine by faith, I then receive him to be mine. ... Things must be, before I believe them to be."[16] Goodwin grounds the order of the Spirit's work of faith followed by sealing in New Testament precedent, theological reflection, and personal experience.

The third point Goodwin makes from the sealing in the text is that Jesus Christ is the virtual cause in whom we are sealed. As Paul puts it, it is in him that we are sealed. The two little words "in whom" are loaded with significance. Sealing, being a distinct benefit from faith, is found in Christ, like all benefits. When the Spirit seals he makes plain to us that we are in Christ. And when we are sealed it is by virtue of Christ, in the sense that whatever God works on us he did to Christ first. Speaking of Jesus, Goodwin claims,

> Though he had the assurance of faith that he was the Son of God, he knew it out of the Scriptures by reading all the prophets; yes, and as Adam had it written in his heart that he was the son of God, so Christ had the like instinct and law in his spirit that he was the Son of God. Yet to have it sealed to him with joy unspeakable and glorious, by the witness of all the three Persons, this was deferred to the time of his baptism.[17]

We can be as assured of our standing with God through the Spirit's sealing, as Jesus was when he audibly heard of the Father's favor and the Spirit, descending like a dove, sealed him.

The fourth consideration is the person who is the sealer. The efficient cause by whom we are sealed is none other than the Holy Spirit, whose unique work is that of comfort. In fact, assurance is his work alone. Even evidence of grace in us is only comforting insofar as the Spirit witnesses to it. The Spirit is given two descriptors in this passage: "Spirit *of promise*" and the "*Holy* Spirit." He is the Spirit of promise as the promised sealer and comforter of those who believe. As Jesus Christ was the great promise of the Old Testament, the Spirit is the unparalleled promise of the New Testament. Goodwin reminds us, "Men had the Spirit to work faith before, they had faith under the Old Testament. But for the Spirit to come and work joy unspeakable and glorious in ordinary believers, was not till Jesus Christ himself was glorified." Indeed, it seems to have been the ordinary experience of Christians in the New Testament churches. It certainly was at the church in Ephesus, for Paul speaks of sealing in the past tense, collectively. Why the experience is now rare, Goodwin does not definitively say, but suggests, "The reason men attain it not, is because they rest in other assurance, and they do not aim at this; they content themselves with bare believing, and that their consciences are quieted."[18]

The Spirit is called the Spirit of promise because he also brings a promise home to the heart. Goodwin exegetically grounds this again in Jesus' baptism and John 14, while clearly denying that the Spirit works or seals apart from the word. If the Spirit were to work apart from Scripture, this would be extrabiblical revelation, referred to as "enthusiasm" in the seventeenth century, and this claim was condemned by Goodwin and the larger Reformed tradition. In his own words,

> All your revelations that are without the Word, or would draw you from the Word, are naught and dangerous. We do not speak for enthusiasms; it is the Spirit applying the Word to the heart that we speak of. It is not to write new Scripture, to make words, to be guided by the Holy Ghost without the Word. No, we detest all such; but it is to draw you to the Word; he fastens the Word upon your hearts, seals you by a promise.[19]

The Spirit is the Spirit of promise, yet also described as the Holy Spirit.

The adjective "holy" refers not to the Spirit himself, but to the effect of the Spirit's sealing. The Spirit seals only those who are holy (John 14:21). Goodwin writes, "God does not put these cordials into a foul stomach; and when a man has these, they make him wonderfully holy." Thus the believer must attain a level of holiness before the experience of sealing, which itself motivates more holiness. It is "a new conversion, it will make a man differ from himself in what he was before in that manner almost as conversion does before he was converted. There is a new edition of all a man's graces, when the Holy Ghost comes as sealer. ... It makes a man work for God ten times more than before. ... It is the next thing to heaven, therefore it must needs make a man heavenly."[20] The person who seals is the Holy Spirit of promise.

Finally, we come to Goodwin's fifth and final point about sealing, which concerns the people who are sealed, specifically those who have the Holy Spirit as an earnest or down payment. Paul in Ephesians 1 speaks of the Father's election, the Son's redemption, and now in verse 14 the Spirit as an earnest of our inheritance. As an earnest, the Spirit is not so much a pledge or a pawn, but a down payment. He is part of a payment, in kind, of the full payment, which is everything that comes with the promise of eternal life in Christ Jesus. Therefore, his sealing work and his function as an earnest overlap but are not synonymous. The Spirit as an earnest conveys not just assurance, but the third person of the Trinity himself with all of the accompanying promises. The Spirit, being God himself, distinct from his benefits, is the greatest earnest that can be conceived.

All of this said, Goodwin is still convinced that the Spirit as an earnest "in a more proper sense ... is spoken in respect of the work of assurance which the Holy Ghost works in us." As a sealer, the Spirit is an earnest. Distinguishing between the sealing and earnest, Goodwin concludes, "There is a work both upon the understanding and upon the will. By the one a man knows his estate in grace, his understanding fully convinced of it, the will and affections do taste the sweetness of it beforehand." When the Spirit seals in the believer's mind the unshakable confidence of salvation, as an earnest, he "is giving you part in hand, part of that joy and comfort, that taste of heaven," and "it is not a bare conviction that a man shall go to heaven, but God tells him in part what heaven is, and lets the soul feel it. There is nothing sweeter than the love of God, and the tasting of that sweetness in the earnest of the inheritance."[21] The inheritance is God himself, which we receive at the "redemption of the purchased possession," redemption, not in the sense of paying the price, but rather applying the payment in full. The purchased possession is at the same time heaven, our inheritance, and the church, which is God's. All this, like the consummation of all things, is to the praise of God's glory.

Goodwin's key exegetical moves in Ephesians 1:11–14 are as follows. First, he distinguishes sealing from faith. Sealing is the work of the Spirit, not the gift of the Spirit himself, which is common to all believers and received at conversion. Second, this sealing comes subsequent to salvation, which necessarily means it is not essential for salvation. In fact, many never experience the sealing of the Spirit. Third, the sealing comes in Christ as a benefit only given to those who are united to him. Fourth, the Spirit alone is the agent of this sealing in his role as Comforter, the very name given to him by Jesus. Last, the sealing brings with it assurance of one's inheritance. It is a taste of heaven accompanied by joy unspeakable and full of glory. It is a total confidence, a complete assurance beyond reason and evidence. It is felt in the soul as the immediate witness of the Holy Spirit, resulting in unshakable certainty of being covered by Christ's blood.

SYSTEMATIC THEOLOGY

Goodwin did not leave us with a complete system of doctrine, but in his *The Object and Acts of Justifying Faith* is a systematic treatment of his theology of assurance. In short, Goodwin argues that faith and assurance are distinct and that assurance is possible as a result of the witness of the Holy Spirit. His claim that justifying faith does not necessarily contain "prevailing assurance," which he defines as "assurance as overpowers doubts and sense to the contrary, so as, in the believer's knowledge, he is able to say, Christ is mine, and my sins are forgiven," is essential both biblically and pastorally.[22] Think of the Beatitudes, where Jesus teaches that the poor in Spirit, the meek, the mourning, those who hunger and thirst after righteousness are blessed. In Goodwin's view, all of these conditions imply a lack of assurance. And Jesus is certainly not teaching they are conditions of justification, but rather things believers experience. Or consider the parable of the tax collector and the Pharisee—the poor publican, who Jesus says was justified, "standing far off, would not even lift his eyes to heaven, but beat his breast, saying, 'God, be merciful to me, a sinner!'" (Luke 18:13). This sinner had faith and felt far from God and excruciatingly in need of mercy for access to him, whereas the Pharisee looked on him with false humility, deceiving himself about his relationship with God. The distinction between faith and assurance is both biblical and pastorally critical. It keeps believers without assurance from despair, as well as believers with assurance from looking down on others as lacking faith. The unity of the haves and the have-nots is at stake.

Distinguishing between faith and assurance is also logical, or theologically necessary. Faith does not claim that "Christ is mine," but that Christ is who he says he is and does what he says he does, namely, he is truly the Son of God who atones for sins and applies his righteousness to sinners. Faith is an operation primarily of the will, while assurance is an operation of understanding. For Goodwin, assurance is the reward of faith, not the other way around. Faith unites to Christ and continues that union. The union does not somehow become dependent on assurance. This is why believers can feel deserted by God. Those who claim never to have felt such desertion, Goodwin dismisses as not having lived long enough. He writes, almost sarcastically, "As for those that will say, that faith is a triumphing, and prevailing assurance, I would refer them but to ten or twenty years' experience, which may (if they be not the more wary) lamentably confute them; for they may fall into darkness as well as Job did, and then if they do so, what is the faith they live by?" Doubt is a corruption, and like all corruptions, believers are not automatically freed from it. Christians may even doubt the very existence of God or the truth of Scripture at times. Therefore, assurance must be added to faith, either "by a reflex act upon grace in a man, and then it is experience (as the apostle calls it) which breeds this hope, or by an immediate discovery of the Spirit with joy unspeakable, which has sense and sight in it."[23] Assurance can be derived from evidences of grace in one's life or directly from the Holy Spirit. It is distinct from faith both biblically and theologically, which has significant pastoral implications.

Assurance of faith (Heb 10:22) is possible and comes via six witnesses. Goodwin draws this insight from *the* New Testament book devoted to assurance, specifically, 1 John 5:7–8, which he translates, "For there are three that record in heaven, the Father, the Word, and the Holy Ghost: and these three are one. And there are three that bear witness in earth, the Spirit, and the water, and the blood; and these three agree in one."[24] All of these witness together "confirm two records: the one, that Jesus was that Christ, and the Son of God; the other, that we are sons in him, and heirs of life."[25] The heavenly witnesses bring the manifest love of each person of the Trinity home to the heart. When considered, the Father's loving election, the Son's loving substitution, and the Spirit's loving application bring incredible comfort. But it is in consideration of the blood, water, and Spirit, viewed as justification, sanctification, and the Holy Spirit, that Goodwin does the heavy lifting for his doctrine of assurance.

The witness of the blood is the doctrine of justification by faith alone. Salvation is by faith, not according to our own works or merit. The blood of Christ can be applied to the conscience when the guilt of sin makes us doubt or we are tempted to trust in our own righteousness. A believer "still in distress can have, with some support, recourse to this blood, when to nothing else, and finds the faith in it secretly supporting him ... for though faith is not assurance, yet upon believing a man may have some evidence from the work of it, and the effect of Christ's blood in his conscience apprehended by faith."[26] Faith is not assurance, but evidence for assurance. The poor man whose boy was afflicted with an unclean spirit cried out to Jesus, "I believe; help my unbelief!" (Mark 9:24). Clearly, he had some access to the reality of his faith; he was able to discern the work of salvation in himself. Faith in Christ, no matter how feeble, justifies, and that is a reassuring thing, the witness of Christ's blood.

The witness of the water, symbolic of the Spirit's cleansing from impurity, is the realty of sanctification in the life of the believer. In Goodwin's words, "The believer finds that closing thus with Christ changes him, renews him, washes him from the power of sin, puts a new spirit and principle into him, clean opposite to sin, so he cannot sin; he finds a new spring of gracious dispositions in him, still bubbling naturally up, and cleansing, and working out corruptions."[27] Regeneration brings about change in one's life, repentance and victory over sin that cannot be explained apart from the work of the Spirit. First John offers signs by which believers may know they are children of God. One is a heart bent on keeping all of God's commands. Another is actually purging oneself of particular sins. Still another is loving other Christians. These attitudes and actions are categorically opposed to our natural inclinations as depraved human beings, which is why John offers the opposite as marks of wicked people.

Because evidence of grace and natural depravity are mutually exclusive indicators, as different as light and darkness, they are infallible in their testimony. God in his infinite kindness has revealed a multitude of signs as evidence of salvation. The doubting believer may look at the evidence of grace, such as a desire to commune with the people of God, in their life and conclude that God has truly worked salvation. This is classic Puritan fare when it comes to assurance. Where Goodwin begins to diverge from his Puritan predecessors is in his discussion of the third earthly witness, the Spirit.

The Holy Spirit may witness to our salvation directly or intuitively—in other words, his testimony can be unmediated. Goodwin beautifully articulates how the Spirit's work is "superadded" to the witnesses of blood and water:

> The testimony of faith finding ease in Christ's blood, as rested in alone for salvation, is often prevailed against by the guilt of sin, and counter-checked. And that testimony of water is worn out and obliterated by the power of sin, which also strengthens that guilt, so that so the soul has an assurance depending on the prevalence of the fruits of grace in itself, which when the prevalence of that grace and faith is in the soul may give a certainty, yet it is as even the soul lingers after, and waits for a further discovery, and is taught to do so, there is therefore a third

testimony, and that is of the Holy Ghost himself, which is immediate; that is, though it backs and confirms what the other two said, yet quotes them not, builds not his testimony on them, but raises the heart up to see its adoption and sonship, by an immediate discovery of God's mind to it, and what love he has borne to it.[28]

The Spirit makes the first two witnesses operative in the mind and heart of believers, of course, but as Goodwin explains, there is more. The Spirit witnesses himself in an unmediated testimony. That said, as noted above, the Spirit does not work apart from the word, which would be extrabiblical revelation. Says Goodwin, "Though this testimony of the Spirit be beyond the witness of faith or water, and above what the word in any sound or syllables carries with it, yet it is always in and with the word, and according to it, and therefore said to be 'sealed with the Spirit of promise' (Eph 1:13)."[29] It is here, in Goodwin's wedding of the mysterious, direct witness of the Spirit—where the impression of assurance is unmistakable, even if inexplicable, to the sealing of Ephesians 1:13—that he changes the trajectory of the Puritan doctrine of assurance.

FOR TODAY

Few groups in the history of the church have thought as deeply as the Puritans about the assurance of faith. The Church of Rome denied its very possibility, apart from extremely rare occasions of special revelation. To be an English citizen at the time was to be a Christian, a baptized member of the Church of England, or later one of the dissenting denominations. Not all English citizens were sincere believers, of course, which presented numerous pastoral dilemmas. These, among other factors, often stemming from personal experience, made assurance a frontline issue for the Puritans. Goodwin was a giant among them in this regard. He labored so intensely because assurance is a universal Christian struggle, making the doctrine acutely personal and strategically pastoral. A robust theology of assurance remains eminently valuable today.

Personal Discipleship

The onset of assurance comes when the Holy Spirit witnesses indirectly or directly to our salvation. The indirect witness is the result of finding signs of grace in our lives and therefore concluding we are saved. Goodwin calls this a reflex act of faith. The older Puritan tradition spoke in terms of the practical syllogism. In either case, we may conclude, based on our sanctification, that we were elected by God in eternity past and will one day be glorified. The reasoning presupposes two things. One, that salvation is like a chain with many links stretching from eternity past to eternity future, a single link of which implies the whole. Sanctification is one observable link in this life. Two, that victory over sin and positive obedience are impossible apart from the Spirit's empowering. This indirect witness, while only effective because of the Spirit's work, is always accessible and available to us. In light of this, we should examine our lives for repentance, the fruit of faith. We should survey our lives over time for increased holiness. We should study our souls to see whether there is true sorrow over sin and desire to please God. We should scrutinize our motives to reveal whether they end with the glory of God. If such things are a reality, we may be confident of our eternal salvation.

The direct witness of the Spirit is unmediated. It is not based on evidence. It is what Goodwin identifies as sealing. This direct witness is accompanied by glorious joy beyond words, unequaled this side of heaven. The possibility of this kind of assurance should drive us to action. We should be begging God for it, crying out for it in prayer, regularly and earnestly. We should be meditating on what it would be like to know, beyond a shadow of a doubt, that our eternity is secure. We should be actively following after Jesus, knowing that the Comforter will not do his work in a believer in active disobedience. The Scripture is clear about this. A proper understanding of assurance, what we have control over and what we do not, is essential for our personal discipleship.

Pastoral Practice

A proper understanding of assurance is also essential for those of us in pastoral roles. By pastoral, I mean vocational pastors, lay elders, counselors, parents, disciple-makers, and anyone who is coming alongside another Christian and encouraging them in their faith. Discipleship includes pointing people to the evidences of grace in their life, not as an infallible source of confidence, but as genuine indicators of salvation. It demands knowing the promises of God in Scripture and having the skill to apply them. It requires wisdom to discern between doubt and conviction of sin, and how long to let the pain of the latter linger. Puritans thought of pastors as physicians of the soul, and like any other practitioners, they needed practice and experience, but above all a proper understanding of their vocation. A well-developed doctrine of assurance is a must for faithful pastoral practice.

Problematic Exegesis

Goodwin affirms, with the Puritan tradition as a whole, that assurance is distinct from faith and that it may be obtained through the Holy Spirit's witness both through evidences of grace and directly, or apart from those graces. His innovation comes when he ascribes the immediate witness of the Spirit, which Puritans in general acknowledged, to the sealing of the Spirit. His exegesis to wed these two is problematic. Most significantly, his argument hinges on a dubious interpretation of Ephesians 1:13, which puts the possibility of time, even significant lengths of time, between conversion and sealing. It is no mere logical order for Goodwin. This raises a problem. What about the universal terms with which Paul applies this sealing in this context? Goodwin would rebut that sealing was the regular experience of believers in the early church, but did not continue into modern times. His evidence for this is anecdotal.[30] This primary exegetical move for his theology of assurance causes other missteps as well.

The Puritans used Scripture to interpret Scripture, and Goodwin is no exception. He recruits other passages and biblical theology to support his view of Spirit sealing, but they are almost exclusively the experiences of Jesus and his apostles in the narratives of the Gospels and Acts. Jesus was sealed by the Spirit at his baptism, at the same time as his divinity and sonship were confirmed audibly by the Father. At this point in Jesus' ministry, he was unshakably certain about his identity and mission. The apostles were men of faith during Jesus' earthly sojourn, from at least the moment that they began following him because they believed what he said about himself. But Goodwin argues that they were not sealed by the Spirit until Pentecost. Goodwin seems to make the sealing of the Spirit what is distinct about the new covenant and begins to see sealing in most New Testament references to the Spirit. For just one example, Paul's reference to receiving the promised Spirit through faith in Galatians 3:14 becomes a reference to sealing by the Spirit.[31]

The Spirit indwells and performs numerous functions in the life of the believer. Therefore we should be cautious about imputing sealing where it is not explicitly in the text of

Scripture. Further, it is difficult to apply the experience of the apostles and especially Jesus to our own. They were in a unique period of redemption history, the details of which often have no parallels. The exegesis is questionable and problematic.

Practical Warning

It would be totally unfair to lay the excesses of the eighteenth, nineteenth, and twentieth centuries at Goodwin's feet, but his doctrine of sealing opens the door for the two-tier hierarchy of Christians that became so prevalent in evangelicalism. The very idea that believers need to seek a second experience with the Spirit to feel all the benefits of Christ is dangerous in this regard. This experience became known as entire sanctification in Methodism. John Wesley (1703–1791) taught that this came when the Spirit miraculously replaced the inclination to sin with perfect love. We know he read Goodwin because he published many writings by him in his fifty-volume *A Christian Library*.

Numerous parallels exist in the various manifestations of the holiness movement, for example, the Keswick theology with its "let go and let God" approach to sanctification, which culminates in what adherents call the "Higher Life," or The Christian & Missionary Alliance's use of the language of "crisis" and "deeper life." Founder A. B. Simpson (1843–1919) also read Goodwin. In fact, one scholar observes, "heavy underlinings and marginal comments in his copies of Thomas Goodwin's works, a Puritan writer and theologian, suggest that Simpson's view of a crisis of the deeper life found its roots there."[32] Pentecostalism switched to the language of baptism of the Spirit and added the manifestation of speaking in tongues. Such theologies do not necessitate a caste system, but it is an inevitable temptation of the fallen human heart, which results in either despair or pride. Better to affirm the ministry of the Spirit's immediate witness for assurance and detach it from sealing, baptism of the Spirit, or the like. The Spirit is the seal, the down payment of our future inheritance, and he assures us at some times directly and at other times through the evidence of grace in our lives.

Faith and assurance are two different things. Faith includes assurance in the sense that the believer trusts the facts and promises of the gospel are true. Faith believes that Jesus is the Son of God and the Messiah, the fulfillment of the Old Testament. Faith affirms that Christ died in the place of sinners after living a sinless life and that he rose from the dead three days later, ascended into heaven, and left his followers with marching orders to take the good news of salvation to the ends of the earth. Faith acknowledges that there is no forgiveness of sins or an eternity with the triune God apart from the grace of God in Christ, which he lavishes freely on all who repent and accept Jesus' death on their behalf as payment for their sins. Faith rejoices in the opportunity of union with Christ and hopes for it according to the promise of God. Knowing that one has truly believed and sincerely repented, and therefore is covered by Christ's blood, clothed in his righteousness, and reconciled to God, is assurance. After assurance is struggled for, experienced, and understood, it both motivates and comforts, as we will see in the coming chapter.

CHAPTER 4

The Motivation of Assurance

G oodwin returned to England and settled in London in 1641, where he began preaching his Ephesians series. He still enjoyed unshakable assurance of salvation, and far from engendering apathy or presumption, it propelled him in his calling as a pastor, theologian, and public figure. His rise in prominence was meteoric. It is true that he enjoyed a fellowship at Cambridge and was entrusted with Richard Sibbes and John Preston's pulpit at Trinity Church preceding his wandering and exile, but before his going to London, he had spent seven years in obscurity as a separatist. Like the fortunes of so many in 1640s Britain, Goodwin's changed dramatically. He was invited to preach to Parliament in 1642 and was then appointed to the Westminster Assembly.

Goodwin played an outsized role as part of Westminster. He gave 357 addresses in the first eighteen months, making him the most outspoken of the divines. He had become convinced of congregationalism by the writings of John Cotton (1585–1652). In fact,

Goodwin was entrusted with the publication of Cotton's *The Keys of the Kingdom of Heaven*, which argues for the polity present in New England, and he was later offered a position by Cotton in Massachusetts Bay Colony. Goodwin faithfully pressed the independent, also known as congregationalist, view in the assembly, but he spoke to other theological topics as well, especially justification. When he and the independent minority failed to reform the Church of England in the congregationalist mold through Westminster, Goodwin's role decreased and the Presbyterian faction began to triumph.[1]

The year 1650 was the start of a decade that proved to be the height of Goodwin's political and ecclesiological career. It was also the year he married Mary Hammond. His wife Elizabeth Prescott had died in the 1640s, leaving Goodwin with one daughter. Mary had four children: two daughters, who died in infancy, and two sons. Their son Richard died on a voyage to the East Indies as a young man, and Thomas followed in his father's footsteps as a minister. In 1650 Goodwin became the president of Magdalene College at Oxford University. In this position he served and helped the school both academically and religiously. From this post he served as one of the principal architects of the Cromwellian church along with John Owen (1616–1682) and Phillip Nye (1595–1672). Goodwin became one of Protector Cromwell's closest advisors, attending to him even on his deathbed in 1658. That same year Goodwin played a primary role in drafting the Savoy Declaration, the modification of the Westminster Confession of Faith for independency. However, the passing of Cromwell initiated the unraveling of the Commonwealth and eventually the Restoration in 1660. By this time Goodwin had moved back to London, and the end of the protectorate meant the end of Goodwin's public career and his efforts to reform and defend the Church of England.

While Goodwin modeled motivation for the cause of Christ flowing from a full assurance of faith, he also wrote on the subject. Painfully aware of the charge that total assurance leads to complacency in the Christian life, or worse, antinomianism, Goodwin was careful to head these false claims off. He intentionally explained how true assurance will not make one presumptuous, because it can be lost. Rather than excusing unholiness, assurance purges corruption. Assurance in no way makes the believer less resolute in resisting temptation.

ASSURANCE IS NO CAUSE OF PRESUMPTION

Using Psalm 85:8 as a springboard, "I will hear what God the LORD will speak; for he will speak peace unto his people, and to his saints; but let them not turn again to folly" (KJV), Goodwin launches into reasons why relapsing into sin after experiencing God's grace is utter foolishness. The "peace" the Lord speaks to his people is the assurance of salvation. God creates with his speech, and when he declares peace it becomes a reality. As God accommodates perfectly and never stutters, this peace communicated by God is understood and felt by the one being assured. It is tangible, even if not exactly explainable. While it is certainly folly to sin against God at any time, it is especially senseless after receiving reconciliation with God, for a number of reasons.

God never provides assurance before the bitterness of sin is truly felt, bitterness the believer would reasonably want to avoid. Like a child who has been burned by fire becomes painfully aware of fire's heat and makes every effort to avoid it, so the child of God, having been burned by sin, intends to avoid repeating the damage. When a person experiences enmity with God followed by peace, that person will desire nothing more than maintaining that sweet peace that surpasses understanding. The distress of sin is not quickly forgotten. Goodwin uses

David as an example: "Ask David if he will murder any more after his bones have been broken and set again."[2] Psalm 51 makes agonizingly clear that the king of Israel, after he committed both adultery and murder, wanted reconciliation and peace with God above all else.

Further, consideration of what it takes to obtain peace with God reinforces the drive for holiness. In Goodwin's words,

> Reckon what pains it cost you to wash out the guilt and stain which sin had made, what vows and resolutions you made, what bonds you did seal unto, what promises never to return, what prayers and tears, what raps and knocks at heaven's gates before you could get an answer, or God to speak one word. ... Why, is it not folly now to lose that in an instant what you have been a-getting so long, haply many years, and with so many pains and costs?[3]

In other words, peace with God is by grace, but the application of that grace is painful, as it forces out our fleshly tendencies, overcomes our failures, and exposes our shame. After having come a significant way in sanctification and felt peace with God, why throw it all away for the promise of fleeting gratification? It makes no sense, and thus the remembrance of sin and pursuit of holiness motivates continued faithfulness.

A third reason why peace with God motivates Christlikeness is that the assured believer jeopardizes the joy of salvation by sinning, as David describes it in Psalm 51. Peace with God is better than life, let alone sin: "No, not the loss of one hour's communion with God, which in a moment will bring you in more sweetness than all your sins can do to eternity. If all the pleasures of sin were contracted, and the quintessence of them strained into one cup, they would not afford so much as one drop of true peace with God does, being let fall into the heart."[4] The Christian who knows true communion with God knows the bitterness of sin and the excruciating process of restoration, and therefore seeks to maintain this assurance through resistance to sin.

A fourth and final motivating factor of peace with God is that the pleasures of sin are greatly diminished after the believer has experienced true assurance. Think about it, "take them at the best, when they are freshest, and when your palate was most in relish and taste with them, when you were carnal, and before you knew what sweetness was in God, and they then were but poor sorry pleasures." After having tasted and seen that the Lord is good, the sweet and savory of sin turns sour and repulsive. Sin cannot be enjoyed the way it had previously been because the conscience has been cleansed. Moreover, the new man is at war with the old, "but half your heart can take pleasure in sinning; that new man, the other half, is reluctant, grieves for it, hates what you do; and all this necessarily strikes off much of the pleasure." Further, the new man craves the sustenance it has enjoyed, as a "stomach that has been enlarged to a full diet, looks for it, and rises more hungry from a slender meal, now communion with God enlarges the faculties, and widens them, and makes them more capable of greater joys than other men have, and therefore the creature is less able to fill them."[5] The Christian who has experienced God's peace loses some of the taste for sin.

Goodwin is clear; full assurance of faith begets continued communion with God that can only be enjoyed in holiness. When we are confident in our salvation, we fear God most, fear in the sense of respect, reverence, and love. To call him Father and fall into sin is particularly egregious. As Goodwin says, "In times of affliction it is the property of a good child to love God most. In times of speaking peace, to fear God most and his goodness, and to fear offending him for his goodness sake." All of this because to sin as one of God's children is to grieve him. When his enemy sins, it provokes and angers him. To grieve him is more than to anger him, for by sinning, "when he has so far engaged himself to love a man, and expressed himself to him, and set his seal upon him for his," is to hurt him. This is what Paul references when he writes, "and do not grieve the Holy Spirit of God, by whom you were sealed for the day of redemption" (Eph 4:30). Anger is an emotion that can be vented through revenge and getting even. As every decent earthly parent knows, when a child sins, it is not a matter of venting anger, revenge, or getting even, but of grief. When discipline is then needed, the parent says, "This is going to hurt me more than it hurts you," as the saying goes, loathed by every child. God must afflict himself in order to afflict his children. Thus Goodwin exhorts, "Put not the Lord into these straits if you have any love in you."[6] Those who have experienced the assuring love of God fear him and are unwilling to grieve him.

Goodwin claims concisely, "The doctrine of assurance, if not abused, and of God speaking peace to men, is no dangerous doctrine to make men secure and presumptuous in sinning."[7] This is not only experientially true as a child of God, but also exegetically grounded. First John is all about helping believers with assurance. The apostle says, "We are writing these things so that our joy may be complete" (1 John 1:4) and "I write these things to you who believe in the name of the Son of God, that you may know that you have eternal life" (1 John 5:13). The same epistle also says, "I am writing these things to you so that you may not sin" (1 John 2:1).

Further, holiness is no minor theme in John's letter about assurance. He clarifies, "Everyone who thus hopes in him purifies himself as he is pure" (1 John 3:3) and provides this litmus test:

"By this it is evident who are the children of God, and who are the children of the devil: whoever does not practice righteousness is not of God, nor is the one who does not love his brother" (1 John 3:10). Paul reinforces the necessity of holiness when he argues, "the love of Christ controls us" (2 Cor 5:14). Paul's reasoning, according to Goodwin: "This consideration of Christ's love, he having a principle of love in his heart to Christ, he found to be a powerful prevailing reason to persuade him to live to Christ."[8] The possibility of assurance is obvious in Scripture, as is the reality that it does not cause apathy in the Christian life.

ASSURANCE PURGES CORRUPTION

Goodwin employs John 15:1–2, part of the parable of the vine, to inform a larger discussion about how Christians may discern growth in the Lord. Jesus says, "I am the true vine, and my Father is the vinedresser. Every branch in me that does not bear fruit he takes away, and every branch that does bear fruit he prunes, that it may bear more fruit" (John 15:1–2). This makes the question of whether one is bearing fruit or being pruned for more fruit quite urgent. This is only intensified in verse 6, when Jesus talks about the fruitless branches being gathered and thrown into the fire of eternal judgement. Goodwin uses this motif of bearing of fruit and being pruned for more fruitfulness to argue persuasively that growth in the Christian life includes both the purging of corruptions and the increase in grace. He concludes that assurance itself is a means of fruitfulness, precisely because it is one of the things God uses to purge the corruptions out of his children.

Goodwin writes, "By assuring the soul of his love, and shedding it abroad in the heart, and by working spiritual joy in the heart, God also purges his people." As this is the direct working of God on the heart, the resulting assurance is the total confidence that comes with the sealing of the Spirit. Goodwin references Galatians 2:20, where Paul speaks of being crucified with Christ, which happened when he believed that Christ loved him and gave himself for him. This union with Christ in his crucifixion "deadens a man to the world, makes a man crucify that which Christ was crucified for; and this makes a man hate sin, the more he loves Christ, or apprehends his love." This is true in a double sense. For one thing, sin displeases Christ and is contrary to his will. For another, taking away sin was the express purpose of Christ's coming into the world. The end for which he removes sin is eternal life with him. Therefore, "the more assurance I have of another life, and of a better, and of being like Christ hereafter, the more a man purges himself to be fit for that condition."[9] Those branches that are part of the vine, being pruned for more fruitfulness, will crucify what Christ was crucified for, namely sin, out of a desire to remain in him.[10]

ASSURANCE MAKES RESOLUTE
IN THE FACE OF TEMPTATION

Inevitably, Christians fail and succumb to temptation, yet even when a soul is overcome by lusts, it can by faith lay claim to ultimate victory, enabled by the assurance of perseverance. Such assurance courageously responds to the enemy, for "when he has a man down and under him, that man yet spits in his face, and says through his teeth, I shall yet rise and tread you down."[11] This is precisely what Paul does when, overwhelmed and exasperated, he says, "Wretched man that I am! Who will deliver me from this body of death? Thanks be to God through Jesus Christ our Lord!" (Rom 7:24–25a). Assurance of perseverance in no way causes believers to sin more. Otherwise, guilt in this regard could be laid at Christ's feet for his assuring Peter of his restoration following his denials. Goodwin puts it almost poetically when he writes, "Christ knew the effect of this promise would not be to keep him, and preserve him from falling. And he gives him an assurance he should recover. And to the end to strengthen his faith before the sin committed, even with the same breath he foretold he should so heinously transgress, he assures him he should recover from it."[12] Jesus gives his apostle assurance, that he might not be fully overcome by sin.

The apostle Paul claims, "We are more than conquerors through him who loved us," confident because he is persuaded "that neither death nor life, nor angels nor rulers, nor things present nor things to come, nor powers, nor height nor depth, nor anything else in all creation, will be able to separate us from the love of God in Christ Jesus our Lord" (Rom 8:37–39). Goodwin perceptively notes,

> I have feared life and the snares of it more than death, or angels, or devils. As for death, it dispatches a man's sins and dangers in respect of them at once ... but it is life which a Christian is most apt to fear, knowing his own weakness, and the strength of lusts, and varieties of temptations; but here is a man's life insured (as is the merchant's language), and an assurance put in for life, and so against all hazards of sinning, and therefore we are more than conquerors, because in and during those conflicts (which in view and to sense are dubious, and hazardous which should overcome), faith persuades us we shall overcome.[13]

Paul's exhortation is to fight the good fight of faith, with assurance of success. Thus, Goodwin comments, "A man can afore view sins and temptations, as that general did a goodly army of the enemies, and go aside and laugh out to God in confidence of the victory."[14] The general, of course, is Christ, who set his eye to the cross, wrath, and the devil only after claiming that the time of his glorification was at hand (John 13:31). Jesus, "for the joy set that was before him endured the cross, despising the shame, and is seated at the right hand of the throne of God" (Heb 12:2). Believers can have the same assurance when faced with trials on every side, knowing their outcome is secure.

FOR TODAY

Goodwin led by example in the application of his theology of assurance. The unshakable confidence he maintained in his union with Christ, reconciliation to God, and heaven as his eternal destiny in no way made him complacent in his sanctification, lazy in his ministry, or fatalistic and apathetic about his culture and society. By all accounts, he walked closely with the Lord, committed himself to the church, and devoted himself to the transformation of his country. His assurance motivated his holiness, service, and activism. Goodwin is an example for us today.

Assurance Motivates Holiness

The logic that concludes that assurance is an excuse to sin is either worldly or the reasoning of someone who has never felt true assurance. The idea that knowing we are saved is license for licentiousness has been informed by neither Scripture nor experience. Paul heads off such thinking after asserting justification by grace through faith when he continues, "What shall we say then? Are we to continue in sin that grace may abound? By no means!" (Rom 6:1–2a). He leaves no room for an antinomianism that indulges in sin. This immediately follows his reasoning that our salvation is based on the person and merits of Christ and that those in Christ cannot somehow out-sin the grace of God. Such a thing is inconceivable to Paul because of the vastness of God's mercy in Christ. Rather than excusing sin, assurance fuels sanctification.

A military commander assured of victory in war would never pull back from the final battles. When the enemy is outnumbered, outgunned, and outmaneuvered, and ultimate triumph is in reach, is precisely when fighting should be the fiercest, discipline maintained, orders executed, and strategy persevered in. When the enemy is routed, the opposing forces are vigorously pursued. At no point, when victory is in sight and the soldier is confident of it, does he passively watch it happen or sling his rifle over his shoulder and trudge toward home. No, on the contrary, he obeys the commander because his obedience is the means of the assured victory. The same is true for our holiness.

Paul writes, "Those whom [God] foreknew he also predestined to be conformed to the image of his Son, in order that he might be the firstborn among many brothers. And those whom he predestined he also called, and those whom he called he also justified, and those whom he justified he also glorified" (Rom 8:29–30). One of the links in this golden chain of salvation stretching from eternity past to eternity future is sanctification. Sanctification is the assumed link between justification and glorification. It is our experience in this life. If we are predestined to be conformed to the image of Christ, God's will cannot be thwarted. We will be conformed, and partially so this side of heaven. So is assurance possible? Yes. Can we do anything to lose our salvation? No. Does this combination justify sin? Absolutely not. Quite the opposite. As impending victory brings focus to an army's efforts at eradicating the enemy, assurance of salvation heightens the Christian's resolve to kill sin and move ever closer to the guaranteed glorification.

Assurance Motivates Ministry

Similar to the way assurance fuels obedience, it also inspires faithfulness in ministry, whether one is a pastor, Sunday school teacher, nursery volunteer, deacon, or greeter. The list of ministries extends to every area of the church, to all acts of service toward the body of Christ, to all the "one anothers" between brothers and sisters in Christ. Think about all such ministry opportunities boiled down to the law of love for the sake of illustration. John writes, "Beloved, let us love one another, for love is from God, and whoever loves has been born of God and knows God. Anyone who does not love does not know God, because God is love" (1 John 4:7–8). The appeal is directed to a church, "beloved," and puts things in rather stark terms. If we love we are "from God and know God." If not, we do "not know God." There it is. The contrast could not be clearer. God is love; therefore, those who know him and are regenerate love one another. When the pastor preaches, it is an act of love. When the believer with the gift of hospitality opens his home, it is love. When any spiritual gift is exercised, it is love. When the fruit of the Spirit is manifest, it is loving. But God's love not only necessitates these realities; it prompts them.

Goodwin's picture of an earthly child refusing to disobey, not so much out of fear of punishment as offense to a loving earthly father, has a positive side as well. The child who is assured of a father's love longs to please him. I have experienced this firsthand with my five-year-old daughter. She is a crafter, endlessly producing things out of paper, glitter, and stickers with scissors, colored pencils, and glue. Often her creations are for Daddy, and when her efforts are complete, she can't find me fast enough. She gives me her work, looking for my smile and gratitude, knowing full well she will get both. When she is given a task, such as organizing her toys in their designated places, she will often joyfully hum a tune while diligently doing what she has been asked. As soon as she is finished, she calls for Dad to come look; surely I will be delighted and proud of her accomplishment. Whatever

I am doing, she wants to be involved and "helping" me because she knows her presence warms my heart. My daughter doesn't craft or clean for me or "help" me because she is trying to earn my affection. No, she does these things because she is convinced of my love for her. She strives to fulfill her vocation as a daughter, assured of my unconditional love. Similarly, we are faithful in the ministries God has given to us because we know that we are treasured sons and daughters of the King. Our work is an overflow of that confidence.

Assurance Motivates Activism

As we have seen, Goodwin was significant in his historical context. He served as one of the Westminster divines, deliberating over years about what English society would look like. He was a public servant, serving at the behest of Cromwell in numerous roles. He was a college president, working for reform and better education at Oxford University. As he had opportunity, he eagerly busied himself with the improvement of his surroundings, desiring to be leaven in whatever context he found himself in, and he seems to have gone about this business because of his assurance. He put his hand to the plow, confident of his identity in Christ. If he wasn't sure of his standing before God, it would have permeated his thought, but with assurance, he was freed up to endeavor for God rather than work to earn God's affection. Assurance enabled him to let his life's work go and place it all in the hands of God when the Commonwealth failed and Charles II was invited back to take the throne. Assurance relativizes those causes we give ourselves to.

Ours is an age of activism. People identify with a cause, something such as social justice, gender equality, protecting religious liberty, or the pro-life agenda. Whatever the cause is, assuming it aligns with Scripture, the Christian, assured of

God's blessing, can pursue it with confidence. Assured of salvation, God's children can live balanced lives rather than frantically trying to earn his favor. Assured of God's favor, the believer can sleep at night even when history seems to be spiraling in the wrong direction. Assurance brings perspective to the causes we are passionate about and therefore motivates engagement.

Holiness, ministry, and societal engagement cannot be neatly separated, of course, but can all be motivated by assurance in different ways. Assurance is no promoter of sin or apathy. Quite the contrary. The proper relationship between justification and sanctification is central to the Christian faith, as is the fact that regeneration really does bring heart change, an overhaul of our desires. We work outwardly what God works within us. As Paul says to the Philippian Christians, "Work out your own salvation with fear and trembling, for it is God who works in you, both to will and to work for his good pleasure" (Phil 2:12b–13). Or to the Colossian believers, "[Christ] we proclaim, warning everyone and teaching everyone with all wisdom, that we may present everyone mature in Christ. For this I toil, struggling with all his energy that he powerfully works within me" (Col 1:28–29). The grace that saves is a grace that demands as well as enables and ensures. Jesus says, "Apart from me you can do nothing" (John 15:5). The same Jesus who promised to abide in his followers also says, "If anyone would come after me, let him deny himself and take up his cross daily and follow me. For whoever would save his life will lose it, but whoever loses his life for my sake will save it" (Luke 9:23–24). Goodwin is a helpful example and guide for what such a cross-shaped life should look like, as motivated by confidence in God's love.

CHAPTER 5

The Comfort of Assurance

The year 1660 brought an end to two decades of upheaval in England. Charles II was invited back to take his father's throne, and it wasn't long before he consolidated control over the Church of England. The 1662 Act of Uniformity demanded total religious conformity, which he knew the Puritans simply could not abide. Over two thousand pastors lost their pulpits and parishes in what has come to be known as the Great Ejection. As a result, the Puritan prospect of reforming the Church of England from within was over. And Charles didn't stop there. A series of laws in the 1660s made it increasingly difficult to exist as any kind of church outside the establishment. The Conventicle Act forbade unauthorized religious gatherings of more than five people outside immediate family, driving dissenters underground. The Five Mile Act made it illegal for nonconformist ministers to come within five miles of the parishes or towns they previously served, a crippling thing in the days before modern transportation. The Test Act combined with the Corporation Act barred nonconformists from public office and education at Oxford and Cambridge, the only two English universities at the time. Persecution abated as these laws were less vigorously enforced in the 1670s and 1680s, but their effects were not repealed until 1689, with the Glorious Revolution and religious toleration.

Goodwin escaped the worst of Charles's vengeful attempt to snuff out dissenting churches and denominations. He left his post at Oxford and gathered a church in London in 1660, so he didn't suddenly lose his position and livelihood with the Great Ejection. He didn't see jail time, despite continuing to gather with his people and preach, due to his stature and connections. Yet the psychological effect had to be withering. He and his co-laborers in reform were suddenly unable to do what they were trained to do, what they had devoted their lives to doing, namely, shepherd their country toward godliness through preaching and pastoral ministry.[1] Instead, in the final decades of his life, Goodwin gave himself to his local congregation as pastor and to his writing ministry, comforted by the knowledge of his Savior's pleasure. He died peacefully at the age of eighty in 1680, precisely fifty years after his experience of full assurance of faith. We will look at Goodwin's loss in the London fire of 1666 and his death in the context of these two decades of disappointment.

THE GREAT FIRE OF LONDON

The fire started in a bakery, raged for four days, and left destruction of apocalyptic proportions. The heart of London, the part within the old Roman walls, was home to approximately eighty thousand people, close to a fifth of the half-million total residents, tightly packed into the medieval city and living in wooden houses. Roughly seventy thousand lost their homes, and almost ninety churches, including St. Paul's Cathedral, were consumed. The death toll is unknown but estimated to be low. But so much was lost, including half of the library of the aging Goodwin. In his son's words, "In that deplorable calamity of the dreadful fire of London, 1666, which laid in ashes a considerable part of that city, he lost above half his library, to the value of five hundred pounds. ... I heard him say that God struck him in a very sensible place; but that as he had loved his library too well, so God had rebuked him by this affliction."[2] Ironically, the half that was destroyed consisted primarily of general works of literature that Goodwin had moved to avoid the fire, and what remained were the theological and religious works he had left in his home, which was much closer to the start of the fire. He composed *Patience and Its Perfect Work, Under Sudden and Sore Trials* in response to his loss.

For Goodwin, looking forward to assurance comforts in suffering and loss. Assurance is the result of successfully enduring such trials. He builds his idea of patience with multiple short definitions, but his most thorough definition is worth quoting at length:

> It is a constant, thankful, joyful enduring, with perseverance to the end of a man's life, all the trials that are grievous, how great, how long, how hopeless soever as to coming out of them; mortifying and compescing to in the inordinacy of opposite passions, as fear, grief, care, anxiety, which will arise upon such afflictions, with submitting to God's will, for God's glory, and his good pleasure's sake, still blessing and sanctifying God in all, waiting on God, and relieving one's self by faith in what is to be had in God, and from God, in communion with him, and from his love, in this life, in expectation also of that glory which is the reward after this life ended.[3]

In short, patience is steadfastness or endurance. It is wrought, nourished, and maintained through faith and our love for God. Its "perfect work" is its full effect in the Christian life and future glorification.

Goodwin grounds his discussion of steadfastness and its full effect in an exposition of James 1:1–5 with special attention to the middle three verses. The King James Version, Goodwin's version, reads, "My brethren, count it all joy when ye fall into divers temptations; knowing this, that the trying of your faith worketh patience. But let patience have her perfect work, that ye may be perfect and entire, wanting nothing" (Jas 1:2–4). Goodwin's ruminations on these few verses are gold. What James is calling us to here is revolutionary. When the circumstances of life might warrant fear, despair, anxiety, hopelessness, and the like, we are not merely to grit our teeth and bear it, but to rejoice! This rejoicing is to be with "all joy," the highest joy. This is to be done not only after we have received what God has promised, but precisely before, in the middle of the trials. Trials come in different forms, from persecution to cancer, from the loss of a child to the loss of a library, from a broken marriage to poverty. These trials can be sudden and unexpected. We are said to "fall into" them. Of James' almost unbelievable imperative, Goodwin writes, "When their miseries are so great that they cannot be endured, that yet their joy must be so great as cannot be expressed; this is the hardest duty that ever was required of the distressed hearts of men. And yet God would not require it if it were not attainable; and it is attainable by no other principles but of Christianity."[4]

The demand that we must count our suffering and trials as joy, at times an overwhelming demand, is sustained by two maxims in Goodwin's estimation. The first is "that to have our graces, especially to have our faith and patience drawn forth and exercised in us, to the glory of God, is the greatest blessedness of a Christian in this life." Why? Because the grace of salvation is the greatest mercy that we can experience as sinners at enmity with God; therefore, the greatest spiritual privilege for the Christian is to have that grace tested and proved true. Peter claims that the trial of faith is more precious than gold (1 Pet 1:7), the reason being, Goodwin says, "they being tried, and holding to be right and true gold indeed, they have thereupon his approbation upon that trial; and he sets his royal Tower stamp and mark upon them, secretly in this life, and the same will openly appear to all the world at the latter day."[5]

A second maxim follows: "Faith, being tried, works patience; and that if patience have its perfect work, it will make us perfect Christians." Faith without testing lacks patience. Goodwin argues, "The full work of patience in our souls is, of all other graces, the highest perfection of a Christian ... for thereby you will have that grace drawn forth to the fullest length, wound up to the highest peg, which is not done unless temptations be answerable."[6] Trials produce patience, dragging out and developing the other Christian virtues of the faithful, making them as perfect and completely like Christ as is attainable in this life. Patience or steadfastness does not perfect or complete by merely being added to other fruit of the Spirit, like a capstone. Goodwin gets at what James is really saying by contrasting two hypothetical Christians. In the first instance,

> Suppose a Christian to have had the privilege to have lived in the exercise of all graces in a way of acting, or of an active life, as to have lived in sweet communion with God, and to have walked in the light of God's countenance all the day; and also to have had the opportunity of doing good, and accordingly to have done much good in an active way, as having been abundant in good works, holy duties, praying, reading, holy conferences, etc., but yet all this while with a freedom from suffering, so as there was need for, or use of patience.[7]

Then,

> Suppose another Christian, who has been obstructed and
> hindered and kept from such an active life of doing good
> with that freedom spoken of, but the dispensation of God
> has disposed him to a suffering life all his days, and con-
> fined him thereunto, and therein his patience has been
> exercised under all sorts of temptations; and then also,
> suppose that patience, with all those gracious disposi-
> tions of the heart that are proper to it, has had its free and
> full passage though his heart, has had its operations all
> sorts of ways, according as his afflictions have been. This
> alone would so draw out and exercise all graces, and head
> them, that you would say, "this man is a perfect Christian;
> shall I say more perfect than the other?"[8]

In short, patience or steadfastness or endurance is not simply
one Christian quality among others, but rather that virtue that
compounds the others, perfecting men and women of God.

The reality that patience is the perfecting quality of the Christian life is exemplified in the life of Jesus. Our Lord was perfect
in his active obedience. He embodied all the virtues that should
characterize us as his followers. However, the glory of his perfection is placed on his sufferings, his obedience, and his patience.
Recall the book of Hebrews: "For it was fitting that he, for whom
and by whom all things exist, in bringing many sons to glory,
should make the founder of their salvation perfect through suffering" (Heb 2:10). Again, "Although he was a son, he learned
obedience through what he suffered" (Heb 5:8). And again,
exhorting Jesus' followers, encouraging them with his example,

> Therefore, since we are surrounded by so great a cloud
> of witnesses, let us also lay aside every weight, and sin

which clings so closely, and let us run with endurance the race that is set before us, looking to Jesus, the founder and perfecter of our faith, who for the joy that was set before him endured the cross, despising the shame, and is seated at the right hand of the throne of God. Consider him who endured from sinners such hostility against himself, so that you may not grow weary or fainthearted. (Heb 12:1–3)

Paul highlights the same thing when he claims that Christ was exalted because, "though he was in the form of God, did not count equality with God a thing to be grasped, but emptied himself, by taking the form of a servant, being born in the likeness of men. And being found in human form, he humbled himself by becoming obedient to the point of death, even death on a cross" (Phil 2:6–8). Christ's endurance, his steadfastness through suffering, more than any other obedience, rendered him most acceptable to his Father. His active obedience was natural, given he was the perfect Psalm 1 man whose delight was the law of the Lord. Patience in suffering had to be learned. Patience also perfects us as Christ-followers.

Perfecting patience is directly related to assurance when, just a few verses later in James, he writes, "Blessed is the man that endureth temptation: for when he is tried, he shall receive the crown of life, which the Lord hath promised to them that love him" (Jas 1:12 KJV). Patience in the face of trials exercises the graces of God in our lives, such as faith and love, to which God promises eternal life. At the same time, this exercise makes the graces all the more apparent to us and therefore brings confidence in our salvation. As Goodwin says, "Those experiences do work up a hope or assurance of glory to that degree of firmness that makes us not ashamed ... and this is given as the reward of our patience and tribulations, which are but the loss of things

earthly, in exchange for which we receive this hope and beginning of glory." Then he memorably illustrates,

> If you had had all the brass and pewter that was in your
> house, and it had been melted by this fire, which turned
> into gold; and the stones that paved your yards, or the
> bricks or lime that raised your walls, all changed into
> precious stones; your glass windows, that were dissolved,
> converted into diamonds—you would have little cause to
> complain at the loss.[9]

Suffering and loss force us to exercise our faith and love for God
in such a way that they are ever more apparent to us, bringing
assurance and comforting us during trials.

INTO ETERNITY

After twenty years spent in relative obscurity, with the grind of
Goodwin's pastoral and writing ministries, fever struck. The Lord
was gracious to Goodwin in that he only suffered for a few days
in February 1680. He was eighty years old when he succumbed
to death. Robert Halley (1796–1876), in his memoir of Goodwin,
claims, "Death had to him no terror. So far from fearing it, he
rejoiced in the assurance of faith that he was going to enjoy that
blessedness which he had so often and so earnestly recommended
others to seek, and to which for nearly sixty years he had been
hopefully looking. ... No dark cloud rested upon his last hours;
his end was peace, or rather, holy joy and rapture." Goodwin's son
remembers, "He rejoiced in the thoughts that he was dying, and
going to have full and uninterrupted communion with God." He
also observes, "With assurance of faith and fulness of joy, his soul
left this world, and went to see and enjoy the reality of that blessed
state of glory, which in a discourse on that subject he had so well
demonstrated."[10] As Goodwin taught, so he lived and so he died.

Goodwin's last words verify this estimation of a peaceful end. Along with exhorting his sons to value the privilege of the covenant of grace, he said,

> I am going to the three Persons, with whom I have had communion. They have taken me; I did not take them. I shall be changed in the twinkling of an eye; all my lusts and corruptions I shall be rid of, which I could not be here, those croaking toads will fall off in a moment. ... I could not have imagined I should have had such a measure of faith in this hour; no, I could never have imagined it. My bow abides in strength. Is Christ divided? No. I have the whole of His righteousness. I am found in Him, not having a righteousness which is of the law, but the righteousness which is of God by faith in Jesus Christ, who loved me and gave himself for me. Christ cannot love me better than he does. I think I cannot love Christ better than I do; I am swallowed up in God. Now I shall be ever with the Lord.[11]

Goodwin could smile while facing death, even celebrate the prospect, because of his full assurance of faith. He was convinced of his union with Christ, so he did not wince when faced with death. He was confident in his standing before God and his eternal destiny, so there was no need to mourn. Goodwin left this world assured of his salvation.

FOR TODAY

Assurance can serve as an ever-present comfort in suffering and trials, even in death. In Goodwin's mind, assurance comforts not only because eternal confidence relativizes pain and loss, but because endurance through such things manifests our faith and love, adding to assurance itself. Suffering and assurance have a reciprocal relationship in this way for the Christian. We all, if we live long enough, will face suffering, trials, and the prospect of our own mortality, making Goodwin's insights eminently relevant today.

Comfort in Suffering

Since the fall of humanity, pain has been part of life. Eve was promised pain in childbirth. Adam was promised toil and difficulty. Together they were promised relational strife, as evidenced when their son Cain killed his brother Abel due to jealousy. The story does not stop there. The people of God have been a suffering people in particular. Bondage in Egypt, exile, and diaspora were Israel's lot. The church from its earliest days was persecuted; Steven stoned, James beheaded, John exiled, and the list goes on. The church experienced persecution at the hand of the apostle Paul himself before Christ knocked him off his horse on his way to Damascus, humbled him, and converted him. So-called heretics were burned at the stake during the Middle Ages. Protestants and Catholics killed each other in the Reformation era and beyond. Waves of suppression and cruelty crashed on the Puritans in England. Today, the stories coming from places such as Nigeria, Iran, and North Korea are heartbreakingly chilling. Christians suffer greatly around the world for their faith. We in the United States of America may be spared persecution at the moment, but we are no strangers to suffering, pain, and loss.

Even in the relatively free modern West, cancer strikes, jobs are lost, children rebel, marriages break down, loved ones die, friends abandon us, churches split, and possessions go up in flames. Hopes crash and dreams are dashed. What is the Christian to do? Take comfort in the assurance of salvation. This is why Paul can say, "We are treated as impostors, and yet are true; as unknown, and yet well known; as dying, and behold, we live; as punished, and yet not killed; as sorrowful, yet always rejoicing; as poor, yet making many rich; as having nothing, yet possessing everything" (2 Cor 6:8-10). It's why Job can cry out, "Though he slay me, I will hope in him" (Job 13:15). We can rejoice in suffering, knowing that our salvation is secure, confident in our standing before God, and assured of our union with Christ. If we know our eternal problem is taken care of, namely, the wrath of God due our sin, it doesn't take the sting and pain out of suffering, but it does put it into proper perspective. The wrath of God dwarfs whatever our present trouble may be, as difficult as it is. Further, whatever it is, God has allowed it, and for the Christian even ordained it for good, for making us like Christ (Rom 8:28-29).

Comfort from Suffering

One of Goodwin's most helpful insights is his highlighting of the fact that trials actually bring assurance when we remain steadfast through them. The test of authenticity is perseverance. Without the testing of faith, a profession, or the claim to love God, is all that exists. Our hearts are wicked and deceitful, and we ourselves cannot know our sincerity, let alone anyone else's. Patience, as Goodwin would call it, in suffering manifests our faith, proves our profession, and shows our claims about salvation to be true, both to ourselves and the watching world. So when the diagnoses come, the loss happens, the disappointment prevails, and the pain is impossible to endure, endure. Stand in the grace of God. Lean into Christ, not away from him. Don't curse God; bless him instead. Don't rage; rest. The result of exercised faith will be assurance.

In his encouragement to the churches of modern-day Turkey, in the face of increased persecution, this is exactly what Peter argues. He writes, "In [your sure salvation] you rejoice, though now for a little while, if necessary, you have been grieved by various trials, so that the tested genuineness of your faith—more precious than gold that perishes though is it is tested by fire—may be found to result in praise and glory and honor at the revelation of Jesus Christ" (1 Pet 1:6–7). The pain is not downplayed. In fact, it is said to grieve and is compared to smelting fire, but it is relativized; it only lasts a little while from an eternal perspective. More than that, it results in a tried and true faith that is more precious than anything this world has to offer, precisely because tested faith is assurance.

How to Die like Goodwin

"I could not have imagined I should have had such a measure of faith in this hour; no, I could never have imagined it. My bow abides in strength. ... Now I shall ever be with the Lord" were Goodwin's last words.[12] I want to die with that kind of confidence in my future, an unshakable certainty in my eternal destiny. Like Goodwin, I want to be surprised by the resoluteness of my faith when the final moments come. Don't you? Goodwin tells us how. As we have seen, assurance takes work and itself motivates work. It takes resolve to persevere through suffering. However, this in no way implies that we earn our salvation or in any way keep it in our own power.

This grace-and-works balance is the consistent witness of the Scriptures. The apostle Peter encourages that everything needed for life and godliness has been provided as a gift, and in the next breath, exhorts us to "make every effort to supplement your faith," with "virtue," "knowledge," "self-control," "steadfastness," "godliness," "brotherly affection," and "love." Thus, he can conclude with the imperative, "be all the more diligent to confirm your calling and election" (2 Pet 1:3–10). We are united to Christ by faith, but as Jesus taught, every branch that is part of the vine will bear fruit, necessarily and inevitably, and it is during this teaching he says, "For apart from me you can do nothing" (John 15:5). Paul demands, "Work out your own salvation with fear and trembling, for it is God who works in you, both to will and to work for his good pleasure" (Phil 2:12–13). We work out what God works in. Again, "By grace you have been saved through faith. And this not your own doing; it is the gift of God, not a result of works, so that no one may boast" (Eph 2:8–9). Paul couldn't have been clearer. Then comes verse 10, "For we are his workmanship, created in Christ Jesus for good works, which God prepared beforehand, that we should walk in them" (Eph 2:10). In the end, the grace that saves is also the grace that commands obedience and the grace that empowers it.

Goodwin embodied this faith-and-works understanding and transparently articulates it in his theology, with the related themes of holiness, sanctification, discipleship, and the like. If we want to have his assurance when we in turn meet our fate, we must cling to Christ by faith, trusting in his substitutionary, atoning death on the cross and the imputation of his righteousness to our account, such that when the Father looks at us, he sees the perfection of his Son. Then we need to work like crazy to confirm this salvation with the fruit of repentance and obedience, which is all of grace through faith. Kill sin with intentionality and careful attention to detail, what Goodwin and his fellow Puritans called mortification. Additionally, walk in new obedience to the positive commands of Christ, or vivification. These things make manifest the reality of genuine saving faith, bringing assurance. Therefore, we need to be ruthless with our sin. No secret sins. No harbored confessions. No delayed repentance. No thinking that we might have time to put off getting rid of something in our lives that impedes our communion with

Christ. We need to be implementing godly habits, spiritual disciplines of Scripture consumption, prayer, church membership, family worship, and more. In sum, we need to be leveraging our lives for the completion of the Great Commission. Herein lies assurance because it is precisely what testifies to the genuineness of our profession.

Perseverance through difficulty and trial, added to this fruit of faith—and for some Christians the immediate witness of the Spirit, what Goodwin identifies as sealing—is how one dies like Goodwin, with full assurance of faith. Goodwin taught this, of course, but he modeled it as well. He demonstrated it in the decades of general disappointment that were the final years of his life, when the Puritan cause failed and he plummeted from prominent public figure to provincial pastor and theologian. He further exhibited the comfort of assurance in two acute episodes during those final decades, the loss of much of his treasured library and his last words. To this day, Goodwin remains a faithful guide.

CHAPTER 6

The Legacy of Assurance

Goodwin's experience of assurance and how he articulated this theology has had a lasting impact. For instance, it became the majority view of the Puritans in the later seventeenth century.[1] An introduction to Thomas Brooks (1608–1680), Thomas Manton (1620–1677), and John Flavel (1628–1691), and a brief exploration of the doctrine of assurance in their theologies, will illustrate this majority view. Similar understandings of the sealing of the Spirit continued into the twentieth century with thinkers such as Anne Dutton (1692–1765), John Gill (1697–1771), Howell Harris (1714–1773), Andrew A. Bonar (1810–1892), A. W. Pink (1886–1952), and Martyn Lloyd-Jones (1899–1981).

Not all of these individuals developed their theology of assurance exactly like Goodwin, but they did follow him in separating the sealing of the Spirit from conversion. This was not the traditional Reformed understanding, as we saw with John Calvin (1509–1564), and which was held by Reformed stalwarts such as John Owen (1616–1683) while the tide was turning.[2] In the traditional view, the Spirit is the seal that is given at conversion. Sealing is not something the Spirit does after conversion. Goodwin experienced assurance after a years-long struggle, which was accompanied by a peace that brought rapturous joy. He saw this experience of full assurance as a second, immediate work of the Holy Spirit in the life of the Christian. He found language for it in Ephesians 1:13, "In [Christ] you also, when you heard the word of truth, the gospel of your salvation, and believed in him, were *sealed with the promised Holy Spirit*." To one degree or another, the following individuals came to the same exegetical and theological conclusion.

THOMAS BROOKS

Thomas Brooks was educated at the Puritan hotbed that was Emmanuel College, Cambridge. This was the alma mater of Thomas Hooker (1586–1647), John Cotton (1585–1652), and Thomas Shepherd (1605–1649), pastors who took congregationalism to New England. Brooks shared their ecclesiology but strove to perpetuate his Puritanism in England. He was ordained in 1640, after which he became a chaplain in Parliament's navy during the civil war. After the fighting stopped, he began a pastorate at St. Thomas the Apostle in London. In and around London was where the rest of his ministry took place. He served both at St. Thomas and later at St. Margaret's and was a sought-after preacher by Parliament before losing his position and status with the Restoration of the monarchy and the Great Ejection in 1662. Brooks continued to preach and ministered to a dissenting congregation at Moorfields, apparently with relatively little persecution. His pastoral heart is perhaps most clearly seen in that he stayed in the city to minister to his people during the plague of 1665. The pastor and prolific author died in 1680, his body laid to rest in the famous cemetery for nonconformists, Bunhill Fields.[3]

Brooks's theology of assurance lines up quite nicely with Goodwin's; however, he ties the immediate witness of the Spirit to the New Testament language of sealing less dogmatically. This is likely because he saw sealing as the Spirit's work of stamping the believer with the image of God. Brooks defines sealing:

> To seal a thing is to stamp the character of the seal on it. Now, the Spirit of God really and effectually communicates the image of God to us, which image consists in righteousness and true holiness. Then we are truly sealed by the Spirit of God when the Holy Ghost stamps the image of grace and holiness so obviously, so evidently upon the soul, as the soul sees it, feels it, and can run and read it.[4]

Commenting on Ephesians 1:13, it is clear that he sees sealing as a second work of the Spirit after conversion for the purpose of assurance. Favoring the language of "testimony" and "witness," Brooks echoes Goodwin's doctrine of assurance.

In his treatise on assurance, Brooks defends the proposition that "a well-grounded assurance *sometimes springs from the testimony and witness of the Spirit of God.*"[5] This is a witness beyond the testimony of gifts and graces in the life of the Christian, which the Spirit points to in order to assure us of our salvation. It is an experience of tremendous joy, yet not one enjoyed by all believers. It is a "clear, a full, a satisfying testimony and witness." Brooks argues, "It is a surer testimony than if a man should hear a voice from heaven pronouncing him to be happy and blessed." Of the idea that this witness is a second, motivating work of grace wrought by the Spirit, Brooks says, "The Spirit bears witness to such as hate sin as Christ hates it, and that love righteousness as Christ loves it, that hate sin more than hell, and that love truth more than life. A soul sealed by the Spirit will pull out right eyes, and cut off right hands, for Christ; such souls will part with an Abraham and offer up an Isaac, for Christ."[6] Brooks held a similar view of Spirit sealing and assurance to that of his more famous contemporary.

THOMAS MANTON

Thomas Manton earned three degrees from Wadham College, Oxford, his bachelor of arts in 1639, his bachelor of divinity in 1654, and his doctorate of divinity in 1660. Manton did not spend two decades as merely a full-time student, however. He was ordained in 1640 and preached for three years at the parish church of Sowton before taking a pastorate at St. Mary's in London. He quickly became a leading Presbyterian voice and for the next almost twenty years he could be found at the highest levels of society and influence. He served as one of three clerks at the Westminster Assembly and preached often before Parliament. While he strongly opposed the execution of Charles I, he maintained his favor with Cromwell, proved by several significant committee assignments, including the commission that credentialed preachers and one tasked with articulating the fundamentals of religion to be subscribed to by ministers. This latter committee included Thomas Goodwin, John Owen, Henry Jessey (1603–1660), and Richard Baxter (1615–1691). In 1656, Manton became preacher at Westminster Abbey and pastor at St. Paul's, Covent Garden, both in London. In 1657, he was chosen to be one of five ministers to pray with Cromwell as he deliberated over accepting the offer of the crown.

After Richard Cromwell's failed protectorate, Manton supported the Restoration and was appointed one of Charles II's twelve chaplains. This favor did not last. He was ejected from the Church of England, like so many other Puritans, in 1662. He continued to preach primarily at his house, and the church grew so large that he was imprisoned for six months in 1670. Manton was first and foremost a preacher, and he continued his passion until the day he died. William Bates (1625–1699), who preached his funeral, gave him the title "the king of preachers" and recalled that he never heard a poor sermon by him. Archbishop James Ussher (1581–1656) called Manton "a voluminous preacher" and "one of the best in England."[7]

In the context of his exposition of the Lord's Prayer Manton discusses the themes of the Spirit's witness and sealing, and what we find is similar yet different from Goodwin's theology of assurance. If the child of God is going to address God as "our Father in heaven," a high level of confidence in one's adoption must be present for this address to be sincere. There is a big difference between the effects and fruits of adoption and the feeling of adoption. Manton explicitly states what he means and does not mean by the witness of the Spirit:

> If you would know what the witness of the Spirit is, consider, what are the Marks in Scripture? What graces are wrought in your hearts? How does the Spirit help you to discern those graces, to compare them to the rule, to make accordingly in these things a determination of our condition? And what joy and peace you then have wrought in your hearts by the Holy Ghost? For an immediate testimony of the Spirit, the Scripture knows no such thing. All other is but Delusion, besides this.[8]

Manton couldn't be further from Goodwin on this point. The Spirit's witness is not unmediated, but rather coupled with the fruit of faith in our lives, the effects of grace. Yet, like Goodwin, he sees the Spirit's sealing as a second work following conversion. It is "by the Spirit's work, and the Spirit's inhabitation, we know whether we are the children of God, or not ... because of those graces wrought in us. And this is called the seal of the Spirit."[9] By necessity, sealing is subsequent to conversion because it relies on our sanctification, the evidence of grace. While far from Goodwin on what the sealing of the Spirit means, Manton and Goodwin agreed on the fundamental shift away from the historic position, namely, that sealing brings assurance at some point after conversion.

JOHN FLAVEL

John Flavel had the most eventful life of our Puritan trio. He was the son of a Puritan minister, Richard Flavel, who ultimately died of the plague in 1665 in prison for his nonconformity. The young Flavel went to University College, Oxford, and was ordained in 1650. He served for a number of years in Diptford before settling into the ministry he is remembered for at Dartmouth. He was ejected from his pulpit in 1662, which was the beginning of an intense covert ministry. Flavel preached secretly in homes, remote forests, secluded neighborhoods, even an island that was only exposed at low tide. Once he disguised himself as a woman in order to meet his people for teaching and baptisms. One time, when he was being pursued by the authorities, he launched his horse into the sea and narrowly escaped arrest by swimming through treacherous rocks to reach Slapton Sands. Another time, when preaching deep in the woods, under cover of darkness, soldiers charged the gathering. The church members scattered, and while some were caught and fined, others brought Flavel to an alternative location where he finished his sermon. This sort of thing continued until 1687, with only a brief respite in 1672–1673, when the king gave groups such as the Puritans freedom to worship.

In 1687, James II gave freedom of worship once again, which was then reinforced by the Glorious Revolution in 1688 and the toleration that came with it. When Flavel was finally allowed to preach publicly again, his people built a large church building, where he finished well the last four years of a life devoted to ministry. His congregation loved him. One of his church members reflected on his pastor,

> I could say much, though not enough of the excellency of his preaching; of his seasonable, suitable, and spiritual matter; of his plain expositions of Scripture; his talking method, his genuine and natural deductions, his convincing arguments, his clear and powerful demonstrations, his heart-searching applications, and his comfortable supports to those that were afflicted in conscience. In short, that person must have a very soft head, or a very hard heart, or both, that could sit under his ministry unaffected.

Flavel had a depth to his spiritual experience and his ministry was fueled by his full assurance of faith, which flowed from the Spirit's sealing.[10]

Although he was significantly younger than Goodwin, entering ministry in 1650 while the Westminster Assembly was still in session, the debates surrounding and the development of the doctrine of assurance were part of Flavel's historical context. While he taught that Spirit sealing was associated with assurance and subsequent to conversion, he had a nuanced understanding of the immediacy and extraordinary experience of this assurance. He defines sealing as the Spirit's work of "giving a sure and certain testimony to the reality of that work of grace he has wrought in our souls, and to our interest in Christ and the promises, thereby satisfying our fears and doubts about our estate and condition." He declares, "The privilege of sealing follows the duty of believing."[11] At the same time, Flavel believed that Christians were objectively sealed by the Spirit at conversion and that it was the subjective awareness of this sealing that was most often experienced afterward.[12]

Like Goodwin, Flavel's experience of sealing was extraordinary, but unlike his predecessor, he did not insist that it had to be this way. One day, while Flavel was on his horse, he lost track of time and his nose began to bleed. Out of nowhere, his thoughts were filled with spiritual things and the joy of heaven. He had been praying for assurance and the Lord answered, the Spirit sealing him in that moment. While Flavel's experience was extraordinary, he believed that others experienced sealing in an ordinary way, through prayer, self-examination, and Scripture meditation, without a disorienting emotional experience.[13] However sealing was experienced, whether extraordinary or ordinary, Flavel believed that it brought the joy of assurance. He reflects that sealing

> has the very scent and taste of heaven in it, and there is but a gradual difference between it and the joy of heaven. This joy of the Holy Ghost is a spiritual cheerfulness streaming through the soul of a believer upon the Spirit's testimony, which clears his interest in Christ, and glory. No sooner does the Spirit shed forth the love of God into the believer's heart, but it streams and overflows with joy. ... The soul is transported with joy, ravished with the glory and excellency of Christ.[14]

While sharing a similar experience with Goodwin, he did not make his sealing normative for others the way Goodwin did.

Flavel ended up much more guarded about the immediacy of the Spirit's witness than Goodwin. He went through phases of development and changes of mind, but in the context of the antinomian threat to Puritan orthodoxy at the end of his life, he stated, "You must only stick to the immediate sealing of the Spirit; which if such a thing be at all, it is but rare and extraordinary. I will not deny there may be an immediate testimony of the Spirit, but sure I am his mediate testimony by his graces in us, is his usual way of sealing believers."[15] Those with antinomian leanings were abusing the fact that they had a direct witness from the Spirit about their salvation and deemphasizing holiness. For Flavel, the sealing of the Spirit was a normal part of the Christian life, but not always, or even often, an extraordinary experience. Usually, the Spirit sealed through the fruit of faith in the believer's life. Same ends, but different means.

ANNE DUTTON

Anne Dutton was a British Calvinist Baptist author and theologian. She was born in Northampton, and her parents were generous in obtaining for her a religious education. They attended an independent church as a family, where Anne experienced conversion at age thirteen. A couple of years later, her longtime pastor died, and his replacement was intolerable, so Anne joined a Baptist church in the area, where she thrived spiritually. In 1714 she married a man about whom almost nothing is known. They moved to London and attended the Baptist church in Cripplegate. It was not long before, in 1720, Anne lost her young husband and returned to Northampton. The following year she was wed to Benjamin Dutton, a clothier who studied for vocational ministry. The pastorate took them several places before finally landing them in Great Gransden, Huntingdonshire. The Lord blessed their ministry, the church grew, and they built a new building, but in 1747, Benjamin perished at sea returning from a fundraising trip to America. Widowed a second time, and with no children, Anne spent the remaining eighteen years of her life focused on her writing in fellowship with her church in Great Gransden.

Dutton's significance does not merely lie in that she was a female theological writer in a day when such a thing was rare, but in the influence she had during her lifetime. She wrote treatises, poetry, letters, and hymns that were widely read. She corresponded with two key leaders of the evangelical revival in both England and America, John Wesley and George Whitfield (1714–1770). As a Calvinist, she publicly challenged Wesley's views on election, atonement, and Christian perfection. She openly supported Whitfield's ministry, and the relationship was reciprocal as he helped with the publication of her work. She also wrote to Robert Sandeman (1718–1781) and William Cudworth (c. 1717–1763), calling out their antinomianism. Other high-profile evangelicals she interacted with were Howell Harris, William Seward (1711–1740), Philip Doddridge (1702–1751), and Selina Hastings, the countess of Huntingdon (1707–1791). She was known and appreciated for her piety, a spirituality that included the sealing of the Spirit for joyful assurance of salvation.[16]

Dutton both experienced and taught the sealing of the Spirit as a second work of grace that brought full assurance. She recalls, "Such was the wonderful kindness of my God that *after I believed, I was sealed with the Holy Spirit of promise.*"[17] Making sense of her spiritual experience of assurance, she quotes Goodwin himself, "that as the foundation of God stands sure, having this seal, *the Lord knows them that are his*: so answerably the sealed believer has a certain *knowledge*, and *assurance* given him *that he is the Lord's.*"[18] Dutton argues consistently concerning the timing, nature, and effects of sealing. Sealing is an experience subsequent to regeneration. She writes, "And as the Holy Spirit, at first, gives us a real possession of our inheritance by faith, so also *after that we have believed,* he further *seals us up unto the day of redemption,* Eph. 1:13, by which he gives us a more sensible possession of it."[19] Sealing is a work of the Spirit; the Spirit himself is not the seal, but the sealer. The result of sealing is full assurance of faith. Dutton was an eighteenth-century proponent of Goodwin's doctrine of assurance.

JOHN GILL

John Gill was the intellectual giant who saved eighteenth-century English Particular Baptists from running off the rails into the deism and Socinianism ravaging other denominations at the time.[20] He was born in Kettering, and at an early age his gifts manifested themselves in his ability to learn languages, specifically Hebrew, Greek, and Latin. While he grew up in the church, it was not until he was nineteen that he made a public profession of faith and was baptized. He was received into membership the following Sunday and that evening preached from Isaiah 53. That went so well that he preached the next week on 1 Corinthians 2:2. At the encouragement and spurring on of those who observed Gill, he submitted to pursuing his calling as a pastor. He did some itinerant preaching in villages around Kettering before settling into the Kettering church. Gill soon went to the London church at Horsleydown in Southwark. He pastored there for fifty-one years. From this post he put forth a positive and comprehensive presentation of the Christian faith. In so doing, he established himself as a model of biblical exegesis and systematic theology.[21]

Gill states his position plainly in his commentary on Ephesians 1:13. After commenting on Paul's statement about belief in the gospel, he argues, "The sealing work of the Spirit after mentioned, and with which this stands in connection, is a distinct thing from faith. ... It is what follows believing, and is a work that passes upon the soul after it; and so is something over and above, and more than faith." The Spirit is the sealer, not the seal itself. Sealing is the Spirit's direct witness, not the testimony of "the graces of the Spirit." It is the "confirming, certifying, and assuring the saints, as to their interest in the favor of God, and in the blessings of grace, of every kind, and their right and title to the heavenly glory."[22] Without perhaps the same emphasis on sealing and assurance in his ministry and writing, Gill interprets this key text in the same way Goodwin does.

HOWELL HARRIS

Howell Harris was a Welsh Calvinistic Methodist and one of the leading preachers of the eighteenth-century evangelical awakening in Wales. He was converted in 1735 but was refused ordination in the Church of England because of his Methodist convictions and principles. He turned to itinerant preaching, and before he became popular and gained a following, he often found himself in very real danger from persecution. He did, however, become increasingly prominent, such that twenty thousand people are said to have attended his funeral. He kept a meticulous diary and preserved copies of all his letters. It is from his personal recollection that his theology of Spirit sealing comes to the fore. He remembers there being several weeks between his regeneration and his assurance of salvation. He describes his sealing:

> Being in secret prayer, I felt suddenly my heart melting within me like wax before the fire with love to God my Savior; and also felt not only love, peace, etc. but longing to be dissolved, and to be with Christ; then was a cry in my inmost soul, which I was totally unacquainted with before, Abba Father! Abba Father! I could not help calling God my Father; I knew that I was his child, and that He loved me, and heard me. My soul being filled and satiated, crying, "Tis enough, I am satisfied. Give me strength, and I will follow you through fire and water." … The love of God was shed abroad in my heart by the Holy Ghost.[23]

Harris referred to this experience of the sealing of the Spirit time and again in his preaching and annually reflected on it in his journal. The possibility of such assurance was a theme of his ministry, assurance that was wrought directly by the Spirit at some point after initial conversion.[24]

ANDREW A. BONAR

Andrew Bonar is probably best known for his *Memoir & Remains of Robert Murray M'Cheyne* (1844), a biography of his friend who died at merely twenty-nine years old. Together they served on the Church of Scotland delegation to Palestine to inquire about the condition of the Jews there in 1839. Bonar was born in Edinburgh and educated at the University of Edinburgh. He was ordained in 1838 but left the Church of Scotland for the Free Church of Scotland during what is called the Disruption (1843). He helped give shape to the new denomination, serving as moderator of the Free Church Assembly in 1878. Along with his older brothers, James Bonar (1801–1867) and Horatius Bonar (1808–1889), Andrew left an indelible mark on nineteenth-century Scottish evangelicalism.[25]

In terms of his doctrine of assurance, Bonar follows Goodwin in his understanding of sealing as a second work of the Spirit. That said, he has a significantly different view on what the sealing actually is. He contrasts the Spirit's sealing with the Spirit as an earnest, using the language from Ephesians 1:13–14. The seal is outward, for others to see and recognize. The down payment is inward, invisible to others, for our personal assurance. The sealing, then, is the Spirit's work over time conforming us into the image of Christ. In an address on the Holy Spirit, Bonar concludes, "The sealing in your case is the Spirit producing in you likeness to the Lord—to the King and to the King's Son. If the likeness of Christ appear in you, shining out in your character, in your life, in your exhibiting the mind that was in Christ in you, and bearing in your person some resemblance to the Son of God,—that is the sealing."[26] The seal becomes ever more apparent as we progress in sanctification. Bonar agrees with Goodwin that sealing is an act subsequent to conversion, related to assurance, such that others are assured we belong to God. While there are precious few other similarities, they share this initial exegetical understanding.

A. W. PINK

A. W. Pink, while obscure during his lifetime, has had an outsized influence through his writing ministry in modern Reformed evangelicalism. After more than dabbling in the Theosophical Society, a gnostic cult in England, Pink converted to Christianity in 1908. Desiring to become a pastor, he attended Moody Bible Institute for a while before taking a position in Colorado. Pink's pastoral, preaching, and teaching opportunities took him to numerous posts, including all over the United States and to Australia, before he settled with his wife in Britain in 1936. First in Hove, England, then on the Isle of Lewis, Scotland, Pink devoted himself entirely to his writing, primarily through his *Studies in the Scriptures*, which he started publishing in 1922. Pink's personality and temperament are debated, whether he was to blame for a seemingly unsuccessful ministry and one constantly on the move. Whatever the case, sadly, at the end of Pink's life, he was not even attending a church.[27]

Pink was a workaholic, to be sure, which is perhaps why his literary output is so impressive. The biblical and theological topics he wrote on are countless, so it is unsurprising that he had something to say about the sealing of the Spirit. While closely related to the Spirit's work of witnessing, sealing is distinct in Pink's understanding. Of sealing, he teaches, the Spirit "takes of the things of Christ, shows them to us, and brings us to realize that we have a personal interest in the same." Again, "The Spirit indwelling us is Christ's seal (mark of identification) that we are His sheep; the Spirit authenticating His own blessed work in our souls, by revealing to us our 'title' to Heaven, is His *sealing* us." This sealing happens "intuitively," as it "authenticates, certifies, and ratifies." The Spirit's aim when he seals is assurance. So far Pink's theology of sealing lines up with Goodwin; however, he makes two qualifications that Goodwin does not. First, he points out, "We do not say that this sealing excludes all doubting, but it is such an assurance as *prevails* over doubts." Second, he extends sealing to the Spirit's operation "inferentially," when he helps us discern marks of grace in our lives.[28] While more guarded than Goodwin and more broad in his definition of the sealing of the Spirit, Pink was a relentless student of the Puritans and was one of the bridges for their doctrine of assurance to move from the late seventeenth to the twentieth century.

MARTYN LLOYD-JONES

Martyn Lloyd-Jones grew up in Calvinistic Welsh Methodism, but did not come to sincere saving faith until his early twenties. Following his conversion, he left a lucrative and prestigious medical career in 1927 to become the minister at Bethlehem Forward Movement Mission Hall in Aberavon, Wales. After eleven years of fruitful ministry, Lloyd-Jones was burning out. He was invited in 1938 to a respite by George Campbell Morgan (1863–1945), to share the pulpit at Westminster Chapel, London. Lloyd-Jones became Campbell Morgan's successor, and six months turned into thirty years. The congregation grew immensely after the struggles of World War II, numbering fifteen hundred on Sunday mornings and two thousand for the evening service. His official retirement led to twelve years of broader ministry and the publication of thirteen volumes of his sermons. In the Westminster Chapel pulpit, Lloyd-Jones established himself as first and foremost a preacher, and as a preacher of renown, he became a leading voice in evangelicalism.

Lloyd-Jones's influence was far-reaching. He helped to found the Banner of Truth publishing house, which was largely responsible for the renaissance in Puritan studies in the last fifty years. He helped establish *Evangelical Magazine* and aided in the fledgling days of *Evangelical Times*. He had his hands in founding the London Bible College and London Theological Seminary. He launched and chaired for years the annual Westminster Conference, which was two days of lecture and discussion on topics related to the Reformation and Puritan subjects. Though he was never formally trained as a theologian or historian, the story of twentieth-century evangelicalism and resurgence of interest in the Puritans cannot be told without reference to the Doctor.[29]

Three occasions in Lloyd-Jones's preaching ministry afforded him the ability to dive, in great detail, into the Holy Spirit's sealing, which he equated with baptism with the Spirit. He preached five sermons in 1955 on Ephesians 1:13b; fifteen on Romans 8:15–16 in 1960–1961; and twenty-four on John 1:26, 33 in 1964–1965. Together these provide Lloyd-Jones's definitive, mature reflection on this second work of the Spirit.[30] Much like Goodwin, what emerges is the understanding of second work of the Spirit following conversion that the Christian experiences. This unmediated witness of the Spirit brings full assurance of faith. For Lloyd-Jones, "sealing is an experience, something God does to us, and we know when he does it." In fact, "Nothing can be more [experiential]; it is the height of Christian experience." This experience "is God's authentication of the fact that we really belong to him."[31] Lloyd-Jones imbibed the Puritans deeply and brought Goodwin's understanding of Spirit sealing into contemporary evangelicalism.

FOR TODAY

In taking the time to survey these individuals from various denominational backgrounds, whose lives spanned four centuries, it becomes clear that the teaching that the sealing of the Spirit is a second work of grace in the life of the believer related to assurance is not an obscure seventeenth-century doctrine. Rather, it largely won the day within Puritanism and found proponents in the Baptist, Presbyterian, and Methodist traditions. Further, it found its way into modern evangelicalism through the giant Martyn Lloyd-Jones. The exegetical move of understanding the sealing of the Spirit to be an act of the Spirit instead of the Spirit himself, indwelling the believer at the point of conversion, is significant for our personal piety, pastoral care, and discipleship of others. If the sealing of the Spirit follows conversion as a second work of grace confirming our salvation, the ramifications for Christian counseling and faithfulness are widespread. The doctrine is alive and well and affecting the lives of those in our churches, and wisdom in handling the universal Christian desire for assurance necessitates an awareness of it.

Conclusion

SIX THESES

Goodwin struggled with assurance of salvation for a number of years after he came to saving faith. He availed himself of the primary Puritan strategy at the time, namely, looking at evidences of grace in his life in order to conclude that he was truly regenerate. This brought some comfort, but not the full assurance of faith that he so longed for. When this finally came, the peace was accompanied by an experience of glorious and almost indescribable joy. From this experience, coupled with his exegesis of Ephesians 1:13, he developed the doctrine of the sealing of the Spirit as a second work of grace, wrought directly on the heart. He worked within and contributed to the larger Puritan discussion over assurance that was taking place at that time. His total confidence in no way engendered apathy, but motivated Goodwin in a life of godliness and finally comforted him even in death. The doctrine of the sealing of the Spirit did not die with Goodwin and the Puritans, but was rather picked up in various ways by their theological posterity. To conclude, I offer six theses that summarize the key themes of our study.

1. SAINTS FROM THE PAST HAVE HELPFUL, CONTEMPORARY INSIGHTS

That Christians throughout church history can help us immensely in the present is self-evident to me, but I recognize that in this day and age not everyone shares this opinion. If you have made it this far in the book, my hunch is that you agreed from the outset. If not, then my hope is that you have been convinced by this study of the life and thought of Goodwin. New is not always better. Contemporary is often not the most helpful. It would be chronological snobbery to develop a doctrine of the Trinity without reference to the fourth century, an understanding of divine grace apart from the fifth century, a view of apologetics without reference to the twelfth and thirteenth, or denominational identity without study of the sixteenth century to the present. The same is true if we were to try to advance a comprehensive theology of assurance without accounting for Goodwin and his Puritan peers. Total agreement is beside the point. Goodwin probes the depths of the human soul and brings a careful reading of the whole biblical witness to bear. He endeavored to provide a pastoral and systematic analysis of human experience, leaving behind significant insight and wisdom. Living and writing in a different world while sharing the same human nature is yet another reason why Goodwin and those like him can serve us so effectively, bringing perspective that is only possible as an outsider. The past is a foreign land indeed, and those who inhabit it have much to teach us.

2. THE ASSURANCE OF FAITH IS NOT THE SAME AS THE PRESENCE OF FAITH

Being saved and knowing that you are saved are two different things. There is a certain baseline, gospel knowledge that the believer must be aware of, to be sure. Things about who God is, who we are, and who Jesus is and what he has done are essential. But confidence in one's standing before God is not the universal Christian experience. In reality, the opposite is true. To Goodwin's point, those Christians who have never struggled with assurance have evidently not been true believers long. Just give it time. The reality that faith and assurance are not the same thing is good news. For those of us who struggle with doubt, it is good news that we don't have to *feel* saved to be saved. It is good news for those who counsel and disciple people plagued by doubt, to be able to say, "Your salvation is not based on the perception of faith but rather on the presence of faith in Christ's finished work. Do you trust him?" The distinction between faith and assurance is good news for our ministry to both others and ourselves. We can rest in the promise that if you confess Jesus as Lord with your mouth and believe in his resurrection in your heart you will be saved (Rom 10:9), regardless of wavering, fickle emotions. Goodwin makes this point clearly and persuasively.

3. ASSURANCE IS ATTAINABLE IN THIS LIFE

Further good news is that assurance actually can be attained in this life. Comfort, peace, confidence, unshakable hope are indeed possible. This is welcome news because, as we have said, the longing for assurance is a longing we all have. Even those not acquainted with the biblical concepts of heaven and hell are aware that physical death is not the end, are aware of the reality of an afterlife. Such notions come from being created in the image of God and the ubiquity of general revelation, and while they can be ignored or suppressed, they cannot be denied. By what means assurance comes is debatable, but Goodwin's main point is that God in his grace enables us to have full assurance of faith this side of glory. The Holy Spirit assures God's people by witnessing to the evidence of grace in their lives. Killing sin, walking in obedience, loving others—namely, Christlikeness—does not come naturally. Such things are wrought in our lives by the Spirit, who in turn uses them to assure us we are saved. Even in the absence of holiness, the desire for it is evidence of grace in and of itself. Where there is smoke there is fire, whether it can be seen or not. While Goodwin goes too far in his equating a single, second act of grace on the part of the Spirit after conversion with sealing, his insistence on the direct witness of the Spirit is on point. There are times in the life of believers when the Spirit does witness to their salvation in an unmediated way. This is not divorced from signs of grace in our sanctification but in addition to them. God assures his children in different ways, but assure them he does.

4. THE EXPERIENCE OF ASSURANCE IS SWEET

Goodwin's go-to phrase, "joy unspeakable and full of glory," sums it up. The only thing better than salvation is confidence in that salvation. It is comfort beyond doubt, peace that passes understanding, indescribable delight in the soul, a taste of the glory of heaven this side of it. Assurance is in addition to faith, it is possible, and it should be longed for and then treasured once acquired and fought for when lost. Assurance is communion with God. If you are in Christ, you can never be any closer to God than you are right now; it is the degree to which you enjoy that presence that waxes and wanes. Assurance comes when we are walking before the Lord with a clear conscience, clinging to his promises, and becoming more like what we will one day be, like Jesus, who enjoys the presence of his Father without hindrance of shame or whiff of uncertainty. It is all the sweeter when assurance comes after a drawn-out season of doubt. For Goodwin it was seven excruciating years. For some it is more; for others it is less. Some foster their assurance; others forfeit it. But those who experience it can attest that it is wonderfully, even if mysteriously, sweet.

5. ASSURANCE IS NO LICENSE TO SIN

Goodwin argues extensively that assurance in no way gives the believer a pass on sin. He is aware of the potential charge that his theology entails antinomianism. It is not hard to see the possibility of abuse. Goodwin, with all of the Reformed tradition, taught divine predestination and the final perseverance in faith of all those God effectually calls. The burden for those with this understanding of salvation is to prove the necessity of repentance and morality for the Christian. This burden is only increased when the possibility of knowing for certain that one has been predestined by God unto salvation is added. To this Goodwin would say that God ordains the means as well as the ends. He also leaves room for false assurance and makes clear that true assurance cannot coexist with willful disobedience or in the absence of repentance. In fact, quite opposite of the idea that assurance might breed immorality, Goodwin taught and modeled that assurance motivates godliness and faithful service. Assurance is sweet, and the sincere believer will not want to lose it because of sin. The child of God will not want to disappoint and hurt their Father with rebellion. Certainty of salvation fosters gratitude, which in turn motivates selfless ministry, with freedom from the fear and anxiety of doubt.

6. OUR THEOLOGY OF ASSURANCE HAS IMPLICATIONS FOR CHURCH LIFE

While assurance is a fundamentally personal thing, it has ramifications for our life together in local churches. For one thing, biblical community is one of God's means of assuring us of our salvation. At baptism, a local church is initiating the individual into the covenant community. The Lord's Supper is then the ongoing sign that we are in right relationship with the church and therefore God. When we eat the bread and drink the cup in a worthy manner, we do so collectively, and our brothers and sisters in Christ are affirming that our claim to faith is sincere. When our faith is undermined with a lack of repentance, the church removes its stamp of approval by withholding the ongoing sign of communion. Thus, the proper exercise of church discipline undergirds assurance. Further, our doctrine of assurance inevitably affects our discipling and pastoral care. When we point people to Jesus and find ourselves in counseling situations, we will encounter those struggling with assurance for one reason or another. Knowing what assurance is, how we come to receive it, and ways we can jeopardize it is essential in such circumstances. The alternative is risking the offer of false assurance or leaving someone in despair.

Goodwin reflected deeply on assurance, from both the pages of Scripture and his own experience, and he did so for his own communion with God and because of his pastoral heart for others. That he left so much of his meditation, biblical interpretation, and theology to us through his writing is a gift. He proves a reliable and eminently worthy guide to thinking about assurance ourselves, something we all desire and all at times lack. Goodwin can challenge us, encourage us, and teach us in significant ways. As a faithful Puritan pastor, the theological fare he has to offer us is always practical and more often than not devotional. Reading him fills the mind, warms the heart, and equips for a Christ-exalting life, a life with full assurance of faith.

Works Cited

Beeke, Joel R. *Assurance of Faith: Calvin, English Puritanism, and the Dutch Second Reformation*. New York: Lang, 1991.

———. "Introduction." Pages 1–23 in *Works of Thomas Goodwin*. Vol. 1. Grand Rapids: Reformation Heritage Books, 2006.

Beeke, Joel R., and Randall J. Pederson. *Meet the Puritans: With a Guide to Modern Reprints*. Grand Rapids: Reformation Heritage Books, 2006.

Bennet, R. *The Early Life of Howell Harris*. London: Banner of Truth, 1972.

Bonar, Andrew A. *Gospel Truths*. Glasgow: Glass, 1878.

Bonar, Marjory, ed. *The Diary and Life of Andrew A. Bonar*. Edinburgh: Banner of Truth Trust, 2013.

Brooks, Thomas. *Heaven on Earth: A Treatise on Christian Assurance*. Puritan Paperbacks. Edinburgh: Banner of Truth Trust, 1961.

———. *The Secret Key to Heaven: The Vital Importance of Private Prayer*. Puritan Paperbacks. Edinburgh: Banner of Truth Trust, 2006.

Calvin, John. "Commentary on Ephesians 1:13–14." Pages in 206–10 in *Galatians, Ephesians, Philippians, Colossians, I & II Thessalonians, I & II Timothy, Titus, Philemon*. Translated by William Pringle. Calvin's Commentaries 21. Grand Rapids: Baker, 2005.

———. *Institutes*. Translated by Ford Lewis Battles. Atlanta: John Knox, 1975.

Dutton, Anne. "Gracious Dealings of God." Pages 1–212 in *Selected Spiritual Writings of Anne Dutton: Eighteenth-Century, British Baptist, Woman Theologian*. Vol. 3. Edited by Joann Ford Watson. Macon, GA: Mercer University Press, 2006.

———. "Inheritance of the Adopted Sons of God." Pages 221–86 in *Selected Spiritual Writings of Anne Dutton: Eighteenth-Century, British Baptist, Woman Theologian*. Vol. 4. Edited by Joann Ford Watson. Macon, GA: Mercer University Press, 2007.

———. "Letter III: On Assurance of Interest in Christ: As Belonging to the Spirit's Sealing." Pages 28–30 in *Selected Spiritual Writings of Anne Dutton: Eighteenth-Century, British Baptist, Woman Theologian*. Vol. 5. Edited by Joann Ford Watson. Macon, GA: Mercer University Press, 2008.

Eaton, Michael A. *Baptism with the Holy Spirit: The Teaching of Martyn Lloyd-Jones*. Leicester, UK: Inter-Varsity Press, 1989.

Embry, Adam. *Keeper of the Great Seal of Heaven: Sealing of the Spirit in the Life and Thought of John Flavel*. Grand Rapids: Reformation Heritage Books, 2011.

Evans, E. *Howell Harris Evangelist: 1714–1773*. Cardiff: University of Wales Press, 1974.

Flavel, John. "England's Duty." Pages 3–335 in *The Works of John Flavel*. Vol. 4. London: Banner of Truth, 1997.

———. "Sacramental Meditations." Pages 378–460 in *The Works of John Flavel*. Vol. 6. London: Banner of Truth, 1997.

———. "Vindiciae Legis et Foederis." Pages 318–78 in *The Works of John Flavel*. Vol. 6. London: Banner of Truth, 1997.

Gill, John. *An Exposition of the Old and New Testaments*. 9 vols. Grand Rapids: Baker Book House, 1980.

Goodwin, Thomas. "A Child of Light Walking in Darkness." Pages 299–350 in *Works of Thomas Goodwin*. Vol. 3. Grand Rapids: Reformation Heritage Books, 2006.

———. "A Discourse of Christ the Mediator." Pages 1–436 in *Works of Thomas Goodwin*. Vol. 5. Grand Rapids: Reformation Heritage Books, 2006.

———. "An Exposition of the First Chapter to the Ephesians." Pages 1–564 in *Works of Thomas Goodwin*. Vol. 1. Grand Rapids: Reformation Heritage Books, 2006.

———. "Memoir of Thomas Goodwin, D.D., by His Son." Pages xlix–lxxv in *Works of Thomas Goodwin*. Vol. 2. Grand Rapids: Reformation Heritage Books, 2006.

———. "The Object and Acts of Justifying Faith." Pages 1–593 in *Works of Thomas Goodwin*. Vol. 8. Grand Rapids: Reformation Heritage Books, 2006.

———. "Patience and Its Perfect Work." Pages 427–67 in *Works of Thomas Goodwin*. Vol. 2. Grand Rapids: Reformation Heritage Books, 2006.

———. "The Return of Prayers." Pages 351–403 in *Works of Thomas Goodwin*. Vol. 3. Grand Rapids: Reformation Heritage Books, 2006.

———. "The Trial of a Christian's Growth." Pages 431–506 in *Works of Thomas Goodwin*. Vol. 3. Grand Rapids: Reformation Heritage Books, 2006.

Haykin, Michael A. G., ed. *The Life and Thought of John Gill (1679–1771): A Tercentennial Appreciation*. Studies in the History of Christian Thought. Leiden: Brill, 1997.

Horton, Michael. "Thomas Goodwin and the Puritan Doctrine of Assurance: Continuity and Discontinuity in the Reformed Tradition, 1600–1680." PhD diss., University of Coventry, 1998.

Jones, Mark. *Why Heaven Kissed Earth: The Christology of the Puritan Reformed Orthodox Theologian, Thomas Goodwin (1600–1680)*. Reformed Historical Theology. Göttingen: Vandenhoeck & Ruprecht, 2010.

Kendall, R. T. *Calvin and English Calvinism to 1649*. New ed. Studies in Christian History and Thought. Eugene, OR: Wipf & Stock, 1997.

Lloyd-Jones, Martyn. *God's Ultimate Purpose: An Exposition of Ephesians 1:1–23*. Edinburgh: Banner of Truth, 1978.

Manton, Thomas. *A Practical Exposition of the Lord's Prayer*. London: J. D., 1684.

Master, Jonathan. *A Question of Consensus: The Doctrine of Assurance after the Westminster Confession*. Minneapolis: Fortress, 2015.

Muller, Richard A. *Christ and the Decree: Christology and Predestination in Reformed Theology from Calvin to Perkins*. Grand Rapids: Baker Academic, 2008.

Murray, Iain H. *Arthur W. Pink: His Life and Thought*. Edinburgh: Banner of Truth, 2004.

Nettles, Tom. *The Baptists: Key People Involved in Forming a Baptist Identity*. Vol. 1. Beginnings in Britain. Geanies House, UK: Mentor, 2005.

Owen, John. "A Discourse on the Holy Spirit as Comforter." Pages 351–419 in *The Works of John Owen*. Vol. 4. Edited by W. H. Goold. London: Banner of Truth Trust, 1965.

Perkins, William. *The Works of William Perkins*. Vol. 8. Grand Rapids: Reformation Heritage Books, 2014.

Pink, Arthur W. *The Holy Spirit*. Blacksburg, VA: Wilder, 2008.

Preston, John. *The New Covenant, or The Saints Portion*. London: I. D. for Bourne, 1639.

Sibbes, Richard. *The Complete Works of Richard Sibbes*. 7 vols. Edinburgh: Banner of Truth Trust, 1973–1982.

Stoesz, Samuel J. *Sanctification: An Alliance Distinctive*. Camp Hill, PA: Christian Publications, 1992.

Watson, Joann Ford. "Introduction." Pages xi–xliv in *Selected Spiritual Writings of Anne Dutton: Eighteenth-Century, British Baptist, Woman Theologian*. Vol. 1. Edited by Joann Ford Watson. Macon, GA: Mercer University Press, 2003.

Westminster Confession of Faith. Glasgow: Free Presbyterian Publications, 1994.

Notes

Chapter 1

1. Thomas Goodwin, "Memoir of Thomas Goodwin, D. D., by His Son," in *Works of Thomas Goodwin* (Grand Rapids: Reformation Heritage Books, 2006), 2:lii.
2. Goodwin, "Memoir of Thomas Goodwin," liv, lvii.
3. Goodwin, "Memoir of Thomas Goodwin," lxii, lxvi.
4. Goodwin, "Memoir of Thomas Goodwin," lxviii, lxx.
5. Thomas Goodwin, "A Child of Light Walking in Darkness," in *Works of Thomas Goodwin* 3:235.
6. This phrase can be traced back to Spanish mystic St. John of the Cross (1542–1591).
7. Goodwin, "Child of Light," 238.
8. Thomas Goodwin, "Of Christ the Mediator," in *Works of Thomas Goodwin* 5:394–95.
9. Goodwin, "Child of Light," 266.
10. Goodwin, "Child of Light," 245.
11. Goodwin, "Child of Light," 246.
12. Goodwin, "Child of Light," 252.
13. Goodwin, "Child of Light," 256.
14. Goodwin, "Child of Light," 268–69.
15. Goodwin, "Child of Light," 276.
16. Goodwin, "Child of Light," 378.
17. Goodwin, "Child of Light," 282.
18. Goodwin, "Child of Light," 289.
19. Goodwin, "Child of Light," 298.
20. Goodwin, "Child of Light," 304, 307.

Chapter 2

1. Goodwin, "Memoir of Thomas Goodwin," lxxii.
2. Goodwin, "Memoir of Thomas Goodwin," lxx.
3. Goodwin, "Memoir of Thomas Goodwin," lxx.

4.   Thomas Goodwin, "An Exposition of the First Chapter," in *Works of Thomas Goodwin* 1:251-52, 259-60. For more on the rapturous joy of full assurance, see Thomas Goodwin, "The Object and Acts of Justifying Faith," in *Works of Thomas Goodwin* 8:397-403.

5.   Goodwin, "Child of Light," 317.

6.   Goodwin, "Child of Light," 3:319-20.

7.   Goodwin, "Child of Light," 3:322.

8.   Goodwin, "Child of Light," 3:323-24.

9.   Goodwin, "Child of Light," 3:324.

10. Goodwin, "Child of Light," 3:325.

11. Goodwin, "Child of Light," 3:327-28. Emphasis original.

12. Goodwin, "Child of Light," 3:330.

13. Goodwin, "Child of Light," 3:331-32.

14. Goodwin, "Child of Light," 3:32-33.

15. Goodwin, "Child of Light," 3:334.

16. Goodwin, "Child of Light," 3:338. "Tower" is a reference to the Tower of London, where political prisoners were held before execution.

17. Goodwin, "Child of Light," 3:346.

18. Goodwin, "Child of Light," 3:347.

19. Goodwin, "Child of Light," 3:348.

Chapter 3

1.   John Calvin, *Institutes*, trans. Ford Lewis Battles (Atlanta: John Knox, 1975), 3.2.4, p. 16.

2.   John Calvin, "Commentary on Ephesians 1:13-14," in *Galatians, Ephesians, Philippians, Colossians, I & II Thessalonians, I & II Timothy, Titus, Philemon*, trans. William Pringle, Calvin's Commentaries 21 (Grand Rapids: Baker, 2005), 206-210.

3.   See William Perkins, *The Works of William Perkins* (Grand Rapids: Reformation Heritage Books, 2019), vol. 8.

4.   Richard Sibbes, *The Complete Works of Richard Sibbes* (Edinburgh: Banner of Truth Trust, 1973-1982), 3:433-34, 443, 455.

5.   John Preston, *The New Covenant, or The Saints Portion* (London: I. D. for Bourne, 1639), 387-89.

6.   Joel Beeke has a discussion of the Puritan trajectory on assurance and diversity within the Westminster Assembly in his introduction to Goodwin's works. This discussion informed my understanding in both these areas. See Beeke, "Introduction," in Goodwin, *Works of Thomas Goodwin* 1:15-22.

7. *Westminster Confession of Faith* (Glasgow: Free Presbyterian Publications, 1994), ch. 8, p. 1.

8. *Westminster Confession of Faith*, ch. 8, p. 2.

9. *Westminster Confession of Faith*, ch. 8, p. 3. This statement is not driving a wedge between Calvin and the Reformed tradition, as some have argued. Calvin never claims that "infallible" assurance is part of the essence of faith, and he conceives of faith as always accompanied by some degree of doubt. The Westminster divines are using more precise categories than were necessary in Calvin's context. Doctrine may develop without contradiction. For the contradiction view, see R. T. Kendall, *Calvin and English Calvinism to 1649*, new ed., Studies in Christian History and Thought (Eugene, OR: Wipf & Stock, 1997). For a rebuttal, see Richard A. Muller, *Christ and the Decree: Christology and Predestination in Reformed Theology from Calvin to Perkins* (Grand Rapids: Baker Academic, 2008).

10. My interpretation of the Westminster Confession of Faith on assurance relies heavily on Jonathan Master's *A Question of Consensus: The Doctrine of Assurance after the Westminster Confession* (Minneapolis: Fortress, 2015).

11. Joel R. Beeke, *Assurance of Faith: Calvin, English Puritanism, and the Dutch Second Reformation* (New York: Lang, 1991), 338–39.

12. Goodwin, "Exposition of the First Chapter," 215, 227, 253.

13. Goodwin, "Exposition of the First Chapter," 224.

14. Goodwin, "Exposition of the First Chapter," 231.

15. Goodwin, "Exposition of the First Chapter," 233, 237.

16. Goodwin, "Exposition of the First Chapter," 239.

17. Goodwin, "Exposition of the First Chapter," 245.

18. Goodwin, "Exposition of the First Chapter," 249. "Bare believing" is a reference to mere belief or intellectual assent.

19. Goodwin, "Exposition of the First Chapter," 250.

20. Goodwin, "Exposition of the First Chapter," 250–51.

21. Goodwin, "Exposition of the First Chapter," 258–60.

22. Goodwin, "Object and Acts of Justifying Faith," 338.

23. Goodwin, "Object and Acts of Justifying Faith," 341, 346.

24. The first sentence of this translation, the clear reference to the Trinity, is known at the Johannine comma. It was an addition to the Latin Vulgate, the Bible of the Middle Ages, and made its way into Greek manuscripts in the fifteenth century. It was included in two significant English translations, the Geneva

Bible and the Authorized Version, or KJV, which were the primary translations Goodwin would have been working with. Modern translations remove the sentence, as it does not appear in the early manuscripts of 1 John.

25. Goodwin, "Object and Acts of Justifying Faith," 361.
26. Goodwin, "Object and Acts of Justifying Faith," 364.
27. Goodwin, "Object and Acts of Justifying Faith," 364.
28. Goodwin, "Object and Acts of Justifying Faith," 366.
29. Goodwin, "Object and Acts of Justifying Faith," 867.
30. Goodwin, "Exposition of the First Chapter," 247–49.
31. Goodwin, "Exposition of the First Chapter," 246–49.
32. Samuel J. Stoesz, *Sanctification: An Alliance Distinctive* (Camp Hill, PA: Christian Publications, 1992), 12.

Chapter 4

1. Mark Jones, *Why Heaven Kissed Earth: The Christology of the Puritan Reformed Orthodox Theologian, Thomas Goodwin (1600–1680)*, Reformed Historical Theology (Göttingen: Vandenhoeck & Ruprecht, 2010), 44.
2. Thomas Goodwin, "The Return of Prayers," in *Works of Thomas Goodwin* 3:414.
3. Goodwin, "Return of Prayers," 414.
4. Goodwin, "Return of Prayers," 415.
5. Goodwin, "Return of Prayers," 415–16.
6. Goodwin, "Return of Prayers," 416.
7. Goodwin, "Return of Prayers," 417.
8. Goodwin, "Return of Prayers," 418.
9. Thomas Goodwin, "The Trial of a Christian's Growth," in *Works of Thomas Goodwin* 3:480.
10. For more on the theme of assurance purging out corruption, see Goodwin, "Object and Acts of Justifying Faith," 354–55.
11. Thomas Goodwin, "A Discourse of Christ the Mediator," in *Works of Thomas Goodwin* 5:325.
12. Goodwin, "Discourse of Christ the Mediator," 325.
13. Goodwin, "Discourse of Christ the Mediator," 326.
14. Goodwin, "Discourse of Christ the Mediator," 326.

Chapter 5

1. Jones, *Why Heaven Kissed Earth*, 50.
2. Goodwin, "Memoir of Thomas Goodwin," lxxiv.

3. Thomas Goodwin, "Patience and Its Perfect Work," in *Works of Thomas Goodwin* 2:438. "Compescing" means holding back or restraining.

4. Goodwin, "Patience and Its Perfect Work," 430.

5. Goodwin, "Patience and Its Perfect Work," 431–32.

6. Goodwin, "Patience and Its Perfect Work," 432.

7. Goodwin, "Patience and Its Perfect Work," 433.

8. Goodwin, "Patience and Its Perfect Work," 433.

9. Goodwin, "Patience and Its Perfect Work," 2:443.

10. Goodwin, "Memoir of Thomas Goodwin," xl, lxxiv.

11. Goodwin, "Memoir of Thomas Goodwin," lxxiv–lxxv.

12. Goodwin, "Memoir of Thomas Goodwin," lxxiv–lxxv.

Chapter 6

1. Beeke, *Assurance of Faith*, 253. This is also one of Michael Horton's contentions in his doctoral thesis, "Thomas Goodwin and the Puritan Doctrine of Assurance: Continuity and Discontinuity in the Reformed Tradition, 1600–1680" (PhD diss., University of Coventry, 1998).

2. See John Owen, "A Discourse on the Holy Spirit as a Comforter," in *The Works of John Owen*, ed. William H. Goold (Edinburgh: Banner of Truth Trust, 1967), 4:351–419

3. Joel R. Beeke and Randall J. Pederson, *Meet the Puritans: With a Guide to Modern Reprints* (Grand Rapids: Reformation Heritage Books, 2006), 96–97.

4. Thomas Brooks, *The Secret Key to Heaven: The Vital Importance of Private Prayer*, Puritan Paperbacks (Edinburgh: Banner of Truth Trust, 2006), 142–43.

5. Thomas Brooks, *Heaven on Earth: A Treatise on Christian Assurance*, Puritan Paperbacks (Edinburgh: Banner of Truth Trust, 1961), 297. Emphasis original.

6. Brooks, *Heaven on Earth*, 299, 301, 205.

7. Beeke and Pederson, *Meet the Puritans*, 407–9.

8. Thomas Manton, *A Practical Exposition of the Lord's Prayer* (London: J. D., 1684), 102.

9. Manton, *Practical Exposition of the Lord's Prayer*, 99.

10. Beeke and Pederson, *Meet the Puritans*, 245–49.

11. John Flavel, "Sacramental Meditations," in *The Works of John Flavel* (London: Banner of Truth, 1997), 6:402.

12. Adam Embry, *Keeper of the Great Seal of Heaven: Sealing of the Spirit in the Life and Thought of John Flavel* (Grand Rapids: Reformation Heritage Books, 2011), 72–73.

13. Embry, *Keeper of the Great Seal*, 82–83.

14. John Flavel, "England's Duty," in *Works of John Flavel* 4:218.

15. John Flavel, "Vindiciae Legis et Foederis," in *Works of John Flavel* 6:354–55.

16. For more on Anne Dutton, see Joann Ford Watson's introduction to *Selected Spiritual Writings of Anne Dutton. Eighteenth-Century, British-Baptist, Woman Theologian*, ed. Joann Ford Watson (Macon, GA: Mercer University Press, 2003), 1:xi–xliv.

17. Anne Dutton, "Gracious Dealings of God," in *Selected Spiritual Writings* 3:27. Emphasis original.

18. Anne Dutton, "Letter III: On Assurance of Interest in Christ: As Belonging to the Spirit's Sealing," in *Selected Spiritual Writings* 5:28. Emphasis original.

19. Anne Dutton, "Inheritance of the Adopted Sons of God," in *Selected Spiritual Writings* 4:281.

20. Deism teaches that God is the creator but is not actively involved in his creation, nor does his providence extend into the history or future of the universe. Socinianism denies the Trinity, the divinity of Christ, and miracles, claiming literal biblicism.

21. Tom Nettles, *The Baptists: Key People Involved in Forming a Baptist Identity*, vol. 1, *Beginnings in Britain* (Geanies House, UK: Mentor, 2005), 196–97. For a thorough treatment of John Gill's biography and theology, see Michael A. G. Haykin, ed., *The Life and Thought of John Gill (1697–1771): A Tercentennial Appreciation*, Studies in the History of Christian Thought (Leiden: Brill, 1997).

22. John Gill, *An Exposition of the Old and New Testaments*, 9 vols. (Grand Rapids: Baker Book House, 1980).

23. June 18, 1735, journal entry, quoted in Michael A. Eaton, *Baptism with the Holy Spirit: The Teaching of Martyn Lloyd-Jones* (Leicester, UK: Inter-Varsity Press, 1989), 30.

24. See E. Evans, *Howell Harris Evangelist: 1714–1773* (Cardiff: University of Wales Press, 1974). Interestingly, Lloyd-Jones pushed for the publication and wrote the introduction for the English version of R. Bennett, *The Early Life of Howell Harris* (London: Banner of Truth, 1972).

25. See Marjory Bonar, ed., *The Diary and Life of Andrew A. Bonar* (Edinburgh: Banner of Truth Trust, 2013).

26. Andrew A. Bonar, *Gospel Truths* (Glasgow: Glass, 1878), 111.

27. See Iain H. Murray, *Arthur W. Pink: His Life and Thought* (Edinburgh: Banner of Truth, 2004).

28. Arthur W. Pink, *The Holy Spirit* (Blacksburg, VA: Wilder, 2008), 150–53.

29. Eaton, *Baptism with the Holy Spirit*, 13–17.

30. Eaton, *Baptism with the Holy Spirit*, 142.

31. Martyn Lloyd-Jones, *God's Ultimate Purpose: An Exposition of Ephesians 1:1–23* (Edinburgh: Banner of Truth, 1978), 262, 269–70, 265.

Subject Index

Scripture Index

Old Testament

Exodus

34:6-7 36

Job

1:8-11.................. 20
3:1-4.....................32
7:15......................32

10:16.....................39
13:15................. 35, 99

Psalm(s)

1 95
42-43.....................16
51 .... 38, 76
85:8 75

Isaiah

50:10-11........... 14, 40
53 115

Jeremiah

23:6 36

New Testament

Matthew

7:21........................ 41
12:31 33
13:20-21................18
18 25
28:19-20................xi

Mark

9:24.......................63

Luke

9:23-24................. 86
18:13 61
19:41-42.................11

John

1:26 120
13:31 82
14 ....56, 58

14:21 59
15:1-2.....................79
15:5 .... 86, 101

Acts

15:7-9 56

Romans

1:19-23...................18
6:1-2a................... 82
7............................14
7:24-25a 80
8:15-16........... 51, 120
8:15.......................52
8:16 52
8:28-29 99
8:29-30 83
8:37-39.................81
10:9 125

1 Corinthians

2:2 115

2 Corinthians

1:5 23
5:7 24
5:14.......................79
6:8-10 99

Galatians

2:20...................... 80
3:1 16
3:14....................... 68

Ephesians

1 ....54, 59
1:11-14.............. 53, 60
1:13-14 ....1, 54, 117

LEARN TO LIVE THEOLOGY ON THE SHOULDERS OF GIANTS

The *Lived Theology* series explores aspects of Christian doctrine through the eyes of the men and women who practiced it.

———

To learn more and order, visit LexhamPress.com